A PHILOSOPHER LOOKS AT SPORT

Why is sport so important among participants and spectators when its goals seem so pointless? Stephen Mumford's book introduces the reader to a host of philosophical topics found in sport, and argues that sports activities reflect diverse human experiences – including important values that we continue to contest. The author explores physicality, competition, how sport is best defined, ethics in sport and issues of inclusion such as disability sports, the gender divide and transgender athletes. His book is written for anyone who is thoughtful, a sports enthusiast, or both, and will deepen our understanding of sport and its place in our lives. This new series offers short and personal perspectives by expert thinkers on topics that we all encounter in our everyday lives.

STEPHEN MUMFORD is Professor of Metaphysics at Durham University. He is the author of numerous books, including *Watching Sport: Aesthetics, Ethics and Emotion* (2011), *Metaphysics: A Very Short Introduction* (2012), and *Football: The Philosophy Behind the Game* (2019).

T0134187

A Philosopher Looks at

In this series, philosophers offer a personal and philosophical exploration of a topic of general interest.

Books in the series

Raymond Geuss, *A Philosopher Looks at Work*
Paul Guyer, *A Philosopher Looks at Architecture*
Stephen Mumford, *A Philosopher Looks at Sport*
Michael Ruse, *A Philosopher Looks at Human Beings*

A PHILOSOPHER LOOKS AT
SPORT

STEPHEN MUMFORD

CAMBRIDGE
UNIVERSITY PRESS

CAMBRIDGE
UNIVERSITY PRESS

University Printing House, Cambridge CB2 8BS, United Kingdom

One Liberty Plaza, 20th Floor, New York, NY 10006, USA

477 Williamstown Road, Port Melbourne, VIC 3207, Australia

314–321, 3rd Floor, Plot 3, Splendor Forum, Jasola District Centre, New Delhi – 110025, India

79 Anson Road, #06–04/06, Singapore 079906

Cambridge University Press is part of the University of Cambridge.

It furthers the University's mission by disseminating knowledge in the pursuit of education, learning, and research at the highest international levels of excellence.

www.cambridge.org
Information on this title: www.cambridge.org/9781108994934
DOI: 10.1017/9781108992961

First published 2021

Printed in the United Kingdom by TJ Books Limited, Padstow Cornwall

A catalogue record for this publication is available from the British Library.

ISBN 978-1-108-99493-4 Paperback

CONTENTS

PREFACE

This is the first book that I wrote during the Covid-19 lockdown and I hope that it is the last. The pandemic gave many of us a pause for reflection and, at least in that respect, it was a good time to write a book. Various degrees of disruption entered our lives and those for whom it was only an inconvenience were the lucky ones. Among the inconveniences was the almost total suspension of sport around the world. This placed me in the unprecedented position of thinking about sport at a time when there was none: the first time this has happened since both sport and the philosophy of sport existed.

A pause for thought is a welcome thing, usually, and the dreadful circumstances gave us all a rare opportunity to consider what is truly important in life. Many reported an intense renewed focus as we battled with crisis, mortality and trauma. Does sport emerge with an increased or diminished importance from these calamitous events? That was one of the questions at the forefront of my mind as I composed the chapters herein. I hope readers will find a few surprises and appreciate the context that generated them. Covid-19 will change the world. We will not return to the old normal. Will it, then, also change sport? I believe that it will. It is incumbent on us now to articulate new visions of how the world could be, and that should include a new vision of sport. There is an interpretive question of what currently sport is. There is now also a more pressing political question of what sport should be. I hope that the topics covered in this book encourage and make a positive contribution to that discussion.

I have been assisted in my thinking, and pushed in unexpected and welcome directions, by Sheree Bekker, who also read and commented on the whole manuscript. I am indebted for this guidance. My thanks also to Hilary Gaskin who first suggested that I write this book. I would like to thank my colleagues at Durham who have provided a perfect working environment, even during lockdown. Finally, my gratitude goes to my family for their support, especially during the time of my own lengthy and difficult recovery from suspected Covid-19.

1   Physicality

Activity

Lift a heavy stone, jump over a fence or run to catch a ball and you will be pleased with yourself. You will have a sense of your own power and ability. You will feel invigorated and possibly a little out of breath. Your pulse rate will raise briefly. You have done something, performed an action, acted, been an actor. Even if your capabilities are limited, as everyone's are to some degree, you will still want to exercise them, preferring to do what you can alone and accepting help only when needed. Catching a ball is a simple but disproportionately pleasing activity. An exercise in hand–eye coordination, it consequently feels like an achievement. Satisfaction comes with a clean take: when the ball smacks perfectly into the palm of your hand, sticking securely.

It is pleasing in and of itself to be active, I shall argue. Everyone needs rest and relaxation, of course, but these have to be properly balanced with activity in order to be enjoyed. Too much inactivity gets us down. Enforced idleness is torture. There are many different forms that activity can take, but to understand the role of sport in our lives, and in our societies, we should start with physical activity that is for its own sake. Although I shall focus on the importance of abilities in sport, my account will reject ableism.

Swimming is as good an example as any to consider in more detail. There are some reasons why it might be necessary to swim but my focus here will be the most common case where someone swims for pleasure; that is, just for the sake of being active. Let us consider the ways in which we enjoy the activity of swimming. There is the sensation of the water on one's skin as one is unfettered by cumbersome outdoor clothing. One is surrounded by water and yet also with a sense of freedom in that medium. The real pleasure then starts when feeling the water slide over your body as you move through the water: when you are properly swimming. The four recognised strokes all consist in cycles of coordinated motions, mainly of the legs and arms, whose movements are synchronised. There is much else to get right too, though: your breathing, optimum head position and so on. Getting the technique right allows you to cut through the water at pace. We see that some are faster and better swimmers than others so we know that the technique can be improved with practice. Some swimmers make it look effortless but this is because they have mastered the technique. They have control over their bodies and know all the small details that can add efficiency. Novice breast-strokers might leave their fingers apart, for instance, as the water then offers less resistance. One soon learns to keep one's fingers closed together so that the hands form a scoop or paddle and that the feeling of resistance is what really matters and is how you pull yourself through the water.

The satisfaction of swimming is not just about con-trol and mastery of one's own body, although that can bring a very great pleasure indeed. In this case, there is also a satisfaction in mastery over the water. One might recall one's childhood, entering water for the first time, and being scared that it could cover your face. Contrast that now with how you can kick off from the side and glide a quarter of a length under the water, knowing to blow bubbles out of your nose as you go. Feeling comfortable and at ease in the water comes from confidence in one's technique and then being pleased that one has conquered a fear and gained mastery over a potentially hostile environment.

The acquisition of new physical skills can itself bring a sense of achievement, even when you cannot yet execute those skills well. I don't mind admitting that I was a late swimmer and even now that I have much to learn. It had long bothered me that while I had developed a good stroke, I still couldn't dive into the pool. I had to climb down the ladder or shuffle into the shallow end off my bottom. I could tolerate the embarrassment but it annoyed me that there was something I was unable to do but which looked relatively easy when others did it. Where did one start on learning an ability like that at my age, though? Did I just need to take the plunge (literally)? Was fear the main thing stopping me? What would it be like throwing myself off a ledge into thin air? Would it hurt when my body hit the water? Could I bang my head on the bottom? Would I be able to get back up for breath in time?

Admitting my vulnerability and taking a few tips from a good swimmer, I one day resolved that I was going to learn to dive. Hence there was a first time when I crouched low on the edge of the deep end, looking into the water below me, arms extended, fingers together and pointing ahead, when I had to be brave and make the leap. The first attempt was not great, technically, but it was enough to realise that the water hitting your chest wasn't too painful. Within a minute I was back out and ready for another go. After a few attempts it felt like it was getting better and I could go straight from my dive into an underwater glide and then come up and start my stroke. I felt proud of myself, to an extent, for having conquered a physical fear.

It was not only that, though. My delight came from a sense of pride but also a celebration of my physicality. I had learnt and controlled my body adequately enough to be able to perform a novel skill. I was newly able to execute a significant physical action: cutting through the air and breaking into that potentially hostile environment. I felt alive, capable, powerful, in control of myself and my surrounds, in direct contact with my world, a human being, embodied.

Extensions

The pleasure gained in exercising one's physical abilities is not limited to sporting activities. One might gain pleasure from learning the quick and intricate fingering of a new tune on the guitar, for instance. A novice might be pleased just from learning to play their first recognisable chord. Playing a musical instrument can be a lot of fun in no small part because it requires skill, usually with both hands and a lot of concentration and coordination.

Likewise, one can gain pleasure in mundane tasks where one successfully completes a complicated operation.

Setting aside employed work, which might bring no pleasure since one is alienated from the product of one's labour, consider a household task performed for one's own benefit. Suppose you bought a Scandinavian flat-pack bed that you are excited to have but then find that there is an 86-step self-assembly to complete. The assembly requires holding large planks in place, balancing components in order to slot them together, reaching around corners, screwing in 104 bolts, turning the whole bed over, and so on. There might be some frustrations along the way but, if the task is executed successfully, some self-satisfaction is likely. This is possible for all sorts of chores, tasks and labours performed not for wages but because you wanted them done. Being capable feels empowering in a range of contexts.

There is a further physical pleasure that can be found in some work, and maybe even some musical or other activities, but especially in sport and recreation. This is the pleasure of a good workout. When I swim I like at some point to go for it hard, to put in a sprint over a length, or to have an extended swim, testing the limits of my endurance. At the end of it, I might feel tired, my pulse and respiration are fast and I can feel aches in my muscles, sometimes even burning sensations. It is pleasurable nevertheless. When one gets very fit, exercising hard can bring feelings of euphoria, a strong physical pleasure mixed with the pain and fatigue.

Apart from the immediate sensational pleasure, there can be a use to pushing these physical limits. As in the case of playing a musical instrument, abilities can be lost through lack of use. With physical fitness, we know that it is not just skills that can be forgotten, but capacity can decline too. Periods of inactivity will see muscles gradually waste, cardiovascular efficiency fall away, weight increase, and it will become generally harder to exercise next time. Activity makes more activity easier and fitness can usually be increased by pushing oneself a bit beyond one's comfort zone each time.

How far can physical fitness be extended? In our own case, we cannot be sure. As most of us are not professional athletes, we have practical limitations on how often and how long we can exercise, so we do not know our ultimate capacity. We can get some hints by extension, however, when we look at what the best athletes do.

There are some skills that require such a level of dexterity that we might think them not humanly possible. Consider Simone Biles' beam routine in which she performs manoeuvres that were previously thought too hard for anyone to execute in a controlled enough a way for competition, such as a squatted triple spin on one foot (Biles has four unique gymnastic moves named after her). Similarly, there will be some acts of endurance that we might at some stage think impossible, such as running a marathon in under two hours. Eliud Kipchoge proved in 2019, however, that this can physically be done, although he did not run the distance in competition conditions. Still it showed us something important and was enthralling in its own way. Biles and Kipchoge push forward those limits of human capacity on our behalf. They tell us something about ourselves not as individuals but *qua* human beings. We human beings can, after all, perform these feats. This might be why we can take vicarious pleasure from seeing others exercise their physical capacities.

The connection between sport and physicality is loose. Physicality is one part of sport; but only a part. And physicality is important outside of sport too. Nevertheless, to understand sport, and our interest in it, we must acknowledge our physical embodiment. Much of what I have said could apply also to activities like dancing, indeed any activity where we use our bodies in a skilled and demanding way. Dancing requires a high level of fitness in order to do it well but can be done to various levels of expertise. With dance, it might be even more obvious that the activity serves no immediate purpose and is done largely for its own sake, for the pleasure it brings. Of course, it is possible that someone dances because they need to get fit or because it can be a social activity and a way of meeting people. But for the most part, I maintain, we dance for pleasure. It is possible to show off, when dancing, and it has long been a convention to dance in order to attract possible partners. Showing off can be more innocent than that, however, since it can be an additional pleasure to display one's capacities to others. We are social beings, after all, and do not practise and exercise our abilities simply for our own pleasure. Just as a musician can take some pride in mastering a difficult piece in private, a public performance adds something. It means that others may not only enjoy the music but also marvel at the dexterity and control on show. Perhaps there is nothing shameful in this showing off. We want to please others. Performing an ability that those others lack is not necessarily a bad thing, which it could be if done in a spirit of gloating. If the ability is exhibited in a spirit of pleasing others, after many hours of dedication in order to acquire the requisite skill, then usually the performance is welcome to its viewers.

It seems that we get this in the case of sporting and recreational abilities too. Spectator sports are for our entertainment and consumption and it would be very rare, even perverse, to resent an athlete for having got so good at their chosen sport. Some professional athletes are annoying, certainly, but that is usually because of their perceived personality flaws rather than that they are good at their sport. Displaying one's physical prowess is not of itself a vice. Gloating or using it to belittle others might be.

We can then have a satisfying complementarity, where it can be a pleasure to show your physical abilities to others and pleasurable to see others show their physical abilities. This is a foundation for sports spectatorship since we should acknowledge that sport is not just about participation. For many people it is mainly about watching.

Being Bodied

Philosophers spend much time considering the nature of the mental and frequently ignore the significance of physical activity. What I have described so far, however, suggests a celebration of the fact that we are bodied beings, able to take pleasure in what we can do with our physical existence.

There is a tradition, deriving from Descartes, which denies that we are essentially physical things. This is appealing *prima facie* because a person is not just their body. The body can survive the death of the person, for instance, even though it usually decays once death has occurred. Might we then also think that the person can survive the death of the body, where death is merely the parting of the soul from the body and where the person lives on as a disembodied soul? There would be a problem with this view, however, if persons are essentially dependent on their bodies, even if they are not identical with them. I support a nuanced version of this view in which we are essentially physical beings and this is a fact upon which the pleasure of exercising physical capacities to a degree rests.

The Cartesian tradition directed our attention towards the nature and existence of mind, but philosophers have started to take embodiment seriously, Merleau-Ponty being a key figure. I am slightly nervous about use of the term 'embodiment'. This suggests that there is a thing, in the body, that has become *em*bodied, when it previously was not; or it is at least possible that it is not in a body. Just as someone without power can become *em*powered, it suggests a prior lack. I am not persuaded, however, that a person can either be *dis*embodied or *un*embodied in the first place, in which case being *em*bodied might also be misleading. In the interests of clarity, then, I will just say that we are bodied.

The claim I make is that it is not merely a contingent feature of our existence that we are physically bodied beings, contrary to the Cartesian view. Descartes argued that he was essentially a thinking thing. He would cease to exist only when he ceased to think, not necessarily when his body ceased to be. He could at least imagine, so he supposed, that he lived a disembodied existence in pure thought.

I am not sure that we should concede the possibility to Descartes too readily, however. It seems like he is imagining the minds that we have received and experience as bodied beings, and the thinking that we are able to perform, as if being bodied were some dispensable component of it, which you could discard, just as you might throw away a ladder once you have used it to get out of a hole.

What if, instead, the causal interactions that we have with others, and with the physical locale in which we are situated, shape our nature and identity not just in the past but on an ongoing basis? Everything that I learn, or that stimulates my senses, has come originally through my body. Maybe I can do maths purely in my head now, but the techniques were originally taught to me in interaction with my teachers. And, even now, so much of how I approach the world is shaped by being bodied. I interact with other people who recognise me and in many ways treat me as a white, middle-aged man. Think of how different would have been the experiences that have shaped my personality and thinking had I been black in a mainly white society, or a woman, or facially different, or much shorter than I am, or brought up in a completely different culture at a different place and time. What I think and how I think is shaped by my situation, which I acknowledge to be a position of many privileges. Bodies have locations and orientations in space and time, whereas thoughts do not in the Cartesian framework (which has some appeal; is your thought that today is Thursday to the left or to the right of your desire to be rich?). And think of the confidence with which I walk down the street because I am an able-bodied man, capable of climbing stairs unaided or jumping over a fence if it is in my way. That shapes my experience and my psychology.

Could I even imagine what disembodied existence would be like? Or does the capability of exercising physical capacities shape my whole view of the world? My bodiment might be inseparable from what Wittgenstein called my form of life. Wittgenstein said 'if a lion could talk, we would not be able to understand it' (*Philosophical Investigations*, section 326). I cannot imagine at all what life would be like having never had a body; and I'm not even sure I can imagine what existence would be like if I no longer had my body. So, to paraphrase Wittgenstein, if a disembodied soul could talk, we would not be able to understand it. We would not be able to relate to or even recognise so different a form of existence. Therefore, while I am not ruling out entirely the possibility of something that passes as thought but without a physical existence, it would be such a radical change from our lived experience that I think our natures and identities would be lost in such a scenario. There would be nothing recognisably us in this disembodied thing.

To be human is to have a body, I say, but this does not require that we have exactly the same body over time. As we know, our bodies can change. I might lose a limb, for instance, and this would change the way in which I encounter the world since others might start to treat me very differently. My sense of empowerment might also change, since there would be things I can no longer do that I used to be able to do. This is not to rule out the possibility that I learn new abilities once my body has changed.

Logically, might I even be able to change my body completely, in one day? Perhaps in the future my mind will be able to occupy a robot body. The possibility raises all sorts of puzzles and difficulties (How easy is it to extract the mind from the brain? What if the same mind were duplicated in more than one robot body?), but I need not go into those issues. My claim is 'only' that it is part of our nature to be bodied, which does not commit to it always being the same body that we have.

A final point on bodily capacities is that we should not think of their exercise as a solely physical matter. People think. And whether it be in dancing, playing music or sporting activities, many of the capabilities that we exercise require accompanying thought. Suppose it is my turn in a game of tenpin bowling, for example. This might be thought of as a simple physical act of swinging my arm and throwing the bowling ball down the lane towards the pins. But this is also a mental act. I first consider my strategy. Where must I hit to get the remaining pins to fall? Should I throw hard or could a slower shot be more controlled and accurate? How many points do I need in the game? Setting that explicit thought aside, though, I also need hand–eye coordination. I am monitoring my actions throughout the action, including proprioceptively. I am not merely an automaton but a free agent whose actions are minded, deliberate, controlled and adaptable. My body and mind are, in this respect, inseparable. The Cartesian view overlooks the extent to which they are integrated. Typically, a physical act is also a mental act; and frequently a mental act is also a physical act.

The Desire for Activity

We can now turn directly to what is the main claim of this chapter, in that it is vital to the account of sport that I defend. The claim is that it is pleasurable to exercise our physical capacities. I should spend some time explaining what this means and then I will discuss an apparent objection.

First, what is a capacity? We use this term, and cognates such as ability, capability, skill and power, to signify something that we can exercise or act upon but which we possess even when it is not exercised. I am not going to make any serious distinctions between any of these cognate terms. Some seem more apt in certain contexts, but it might be that their difference is primarily a linguistic one. They are all associated with use of the word 'can', but this word gives only a rough approximation of what we mean. For instance, when you say that you can jump one metre off the ground, it doesn't mean that you are actually doing so now but that you are able to do so, you are capable of doing so, you have the power to do so, and so on.

It should be clear that there is a close connection between sport and the exercise or manifestation of abilities. Sports involve tasks such as jumping over bars and across sand, pulling oars in a boat, running around a track, scoring goals, knocking balls across grass and into holes, throwing a javelin, stopping opponents with your fists, directing a stone accurately over ice at a target, swimming to the other end of the pool, and so on. All these require that the athlete is able to do something and, in organised sports, exercise their abilities in certain prearranged situations.

13

The athletes will know that here, in this event, is their time to show or prove that they can do what they have been practising to do. Sports will also involve comparative measures of those abilities, showing not just that one can jump over a high bar but that one can jump over a higher bar than all the other entrants, one can swim the distance quicker than the others, get one's stone closest to the target, or throw the javelin the furthest. Hence, we are typically looking for who can manifest the greater ability since most abilities come in degrees. They are not just an all or nothing matter.

That sports measure these abilities seems clear, and I will discuss this issue more in Chapter 2, but I do not want my analysis of the nature of sport to be back to front. Specifically, I do not think that it is a pleasure to manifest these abilities simply because we do so in sport. Rather, my account says the opposite. Sport satisfies a pre-existing want to manifest our abilities where we have that wanting because it brings us pleasure to manifest those abilities. First came the desire for activity, and then came sport as a vehicle for the satisfaction of that desire.

The evidence for this thesis is primarily empirical. First I would point out that people want to manifest their abilities even in non-sporting contexts. Sport seems to provide a codified and often competitive arena in which we can manifest our abilities, but there are plenty of non-sporting and informal settings in which we do the same. I have already mentioned dance, music and work for one's own needs as examples of activities people enjoy performing. Often the performance of such abilities will bring no tangible benefit and seem plausibly to be done purely for its own sake. Second, one could think of the pleasure one finds in being useful and the displeasure of feeling useless. People like to contribute and be helpful, this natural state being compromised in the cases where they feel exploited, as with paid labour, or where there is some form of compulsion. On a voluntary basis, we want to be doing things. Consider the cases where children see an activity performed and eagerly ask if they can have a go. Third, one can consider the great pleasure of learning a new skill. The acquisition of an additional ability is one of the greatest pleasures presumably because new possibilities are opened up that were not there before. I took great pleasure in acquiring the ability to dive into water since I knew that it wouldn't be only then that I dived but that I would have the option open to me for time to come. Similarly, consider the great pleasure of learning a new language. The first two times that one is able to hold a conversation in a new language are thrilling partly because that can be the moment of realisation that you have the ability. After all, we cannot know for sure that we have an ability until the first time or two that we display it, just as I needed two or more dives into the pool to check that the first success wasn't a fluke.

It might be worth contrasting the case of abilities with liabilities, though I won't offer much detail on the latter. We could think of an ability as a power that it is useful to have and a liability as one that it is not useful to have, or worse. Liability has a negative connotation. Typically, one is pleased to have an ability but displeased to have a liability such that one would prefer to retain one's abilities or have more of them but one would prefer to be rid of one's liabilities. One might then argue that just as it is pleasurable to manifest an ability, it is displeasing to manifest a liability. For example, consider a high jumper who is liable to knock off the bar with her ankles when she has otherwise cleared it. She certainly wishes she did not have this failing and is unhappy every time that she manifests it. What counts as an ability or liability is likely to vary by context, however, including sporting context. Hence, an ability to run 100 metres in ten seconds is an advantage for a sprinter but it is no use at all to a horse-racing jockey and, given the necessary muscle bulk, would certainly be a liability.

There is a special case of the exercise of an ability that deserves particular mention. Some call it 'flow'; athletes think of it as being 'in the zone'. I take it that flow occurs when someone exercises an ability to the full extent in which they possess it. It is the optimum performance of the ability. It is not just in sport that one can be in the zone. A writer might feel the same, when their writing is going well, or a lecturer. What seems so enigmatic about flow is the way it vanishes as soon as you realise you have it. If you think you are in the zone, then you are no longer in the zone. How is this possible? Here is a theory. To exercise an ability fully, whether it be mental or physical, one needs to put all one's concentration into its execution. If for one moment one thinks of other things, then that distracts from the performance and makes it suboptimal. And the thought that one is in the zone is apparently one of the most distracting thoughts of all, after which it might take a long time to return to that same place.

This is only a brief statement of the case for it being pleasurable to exercise an ability. Perhaps I could have said much more since I have hardly offered a watertight argument. But I am also mindful of David Hume's statement that 'Next to the ridicule of denying an evident truth, is that of taking much pains to defend it' (*A Treatise of Human Nature*, Book I, part 3, section 16). I would say that everyone is able to confirm in their own experience that it gives them pleasure to manifest their abilities. I don't need to use more words in convincing them of what they already know.

Objection: It Is Not Pleasurable to Exercise Some Abilities

What might be more useful, then, is if I defend the claim against a possible line of objection. In making this defence, we will also come to understand the claim better and will discover a more nuanced but defensible version of it.

The objection is that we have some abilities that it is not a pleasure to manifest and which are not obviously liabilities. Many people are capable of doing wrong and it brings them no pleasure when they do so. Let us assume that a person, A, has an ability to angrily shout at B and that if A manifests this ability, it brings no pleasure to A. Instead, A feels shame. I am ruling out the cases, therefore, where someone takes pleasure in shouting at other people, as an uncaring person might. We can set those cases aside since they would not present a counterexample to the theory that it is pleasurable to exercise an ability. They would be consistent with it. The theory only has a problem if what is exercised is both an ability and brings no pleasure, or the opposite of pleasure, when it is exercised.

The simplest answer to the objection would be that the problematic cases all concern liabilities so it does not matter; indeed, it is to be expected that their exercise brings no pleasure. I do not want to rush towards this solution, however, since I think it is not obviously right. Person A here does seem able to do something, even though that thing is wrong in most contexts. The salient point is that the opposite of an ability is not a liability but an inability. If one lacks the ability to x, whatever x may be, one is unable to x. We cannot deny that A is able to shout at someone if they do indeed shout at someone. Liabilities are a different kind of thing, suggesting more a lack of agency: something in respect of which one is passive or has a lack of control. So we should set liabilities aside and come back to the question of whether there are some abilities that fail to bring pleasure.

To address this problem, I suggest that we need to make a distinction between basic and contextualised actions. To understand the distinction, we must see that our actions typically have different layers of description and significance. For example, one and the same action could be described as any of the following:

i. Moving one's finger
ii. Turning on a light
iii. Disturbing someone's sleep

I am calling i a basic action, since it describes only a bodily movement, decontextualised from its setting or any intentions of the agent. With ii we get more information that allows us to understand something further about the action, such as its setting. The finger was in contact with a light switch. The agent, in moving her finger in that way, was turning on a light. Description ii is more illuminating than i (no pun intended) since ii provides a reason for i. We can assume that this agent would not have moved her finger but for the purpose described in ii. With iii we get more information concerning the context. Our agent wasn't just turning on a light but was disturbing someone's sleep. Moving one's finger does not seem to be a blameworthy action in itself, nor does turning on a light, but if we see that this same action was also disturbing someone's sleep, then we might regard it as blameworthy. Instead of the blameworthy iii, had the same action described in i and ii been in different circumstances, it could have been the praiseworthy:

iv. Showing a visitor the way at night

This means that the information provided by the contextualised description will be crucial in evaluating the moral worth of the action. There might be even higher and more sophisticated levels of description that pertain to this evaluation. For example, was the action described by iii performed because of a prior arrangement in which someone asked to be woken at an agreed time?

With these examples we see how the displeasure of a wrong contextualised action can outweigh any pleasure that performing a basic action would otherwise give in a different context. For example, suppose that A and B are in a friendly game of tug of war, pulling against each other on different ends of the same rope. Both A and B can take pleasure in exercising their abilities, tightly gripping the rope and using their muscles to pull their opponents towards them. Treating the game as a bit of fun, both A and B take pleasure afterwards in having exerted their powers as much as they could. Perhaps A has a bit more pleasure than B, if A is the winner.

But let us change the context of this imagined tug of war. It is now played in anger across a ravine, into which the loser will be dragged and plunge to their death. A and B, we can suppose, perform exactly the same basic actions as in the fun game but this time, I think likely, take no pleasure in exercising their capacities. The loser dies and even the winner, to be realistic, will be traumatised by the experience and likely to feel the shame of survivor guilt.

We cannot see anyone taking pleasure in pulling on the rope in a life or death situation. And this would be supported by a view in which we prefer to understand our actions in the most contextualised way that we can. For example, when asked what someone is doing, we will almost always offer a contextualised answer: they are turning on the light to show a visitor the way, rather than simply moving their finger. We have purposes to our actions and these are understood and articulated in contextualised ways, at levels ii, iii or higher.

This account allows us to say, where someone exercises an ability but without pleasure, that it would be pleasurable to exercise the same basic action in other circumstances; but the wrongness of a contextualised action rids even the basic action of pleasure. We thus have to grant the objection to an extent and provide a more nuanced statement of the theory. The abilities that we exercise in actions are pleasurable only in the right context: A and B enjoy the fun game of tug of war game but not the tug-of-war death match. In the death match, though, it is not as if A and B are getting pleasure from their basic actions, which then just happens to be outweighed by the displeasing context. Even the basic actions bring no pleasure, here; but those same basic actions could, in different circumstances. We should grant, then, that not every exercise of an ability brings pleasure. The main claim of this chapter is to be understood, therefore, as true only 'for the most part', as Aristotelians say, rather than true absolutely. For the most part, exercise of an ability is pleasurable. This is not simply an ad hoc evasion of the problem since I also offer a principled explanation of why the claim does not hold universally. It is not simply arbitrary that some abilities are pleasurable to exercise and some are not.

An Important Lesson for Sport

I might now face the accusation that the foregoing discussion has significantly weakened what was advertised as the main claim. We started with the idea that it is pleasurable for us to exercise our physical capacities or capabilities and sport provides an opportunity for us to do so. The charge is now that I have had to retreat from this thesis and concede that only some exercises of our capacities bring pleasure whereas some do not.

Nevertheless, this alleged defeat should instead be taken as a bigger victory, if our primary aim is a better understanding of sport. In addressing the objection, we became aware of the distinction between basic and contextualised actions and saw how the latter was the key to understanding whether or not we were able to enjoy manifesting our abilities. This is a significant result. Might it be, then, that sport provides a set of contexts in which we have permission to enjoy the exercise of our capabilities and it does so by creating safe environments for their exercise? A fight to the death is not sport, but we could use some of the same basic physical actions that might be involved in such a fight instead in a safe environment in which the loser remains unharmed. All parties to the contest are then at liberty to exercise their abilities to the full and take joy in doing so. By conceding some ground to the objection, then, we have actually improved our theory of sport.

Our task of understanding sport is far from finished, however, and there are still questions to face. Indeed, a critic might be sceptical about the view just expressed that losers are unharmed by the contest. It seems appropriate, therefore, that we move on to consider the issues of competition, winning and losing. This shall be our next chapter.

2   Competition

Self and Other

We began with physicality, looking at personal and individual capacities. These concern oneself. Now we turn to competition, which essentially requires an other. We must consider competition if we are to gain an adequate grasp of the nature of sport since sport essentially involves a competitive engagement between self and other.

In the set position on the blocks, the sprinter has an absolute focus on herself. She has trained and prepared and been through her mental routines, doing all that she can to ensure that she is in the zone for the next ten seconds or so since she knows that to win she will have to manifest her capacities to the maximum. Nevertheless, she cannot ignore that she is surrounded by others who have the same goal as her. She is mentally and physically prepared because she knows that others will beat her otherwise. She knows that she cannot control what they do and her only way to win is for her to do her best. Now the race begins. Immediately, the athletes have a sense of who was out of the blocks quickest. One has the sense that she had the weakest start: a terrible realisation. Yet she must also remain calm and now set about recovering lost ground over the next 100 metres. Another senses that she has had the strongest start but also must not be distracted by this and has now to drive hard to exploit the advantage. Down the track, all the competitors have an awareness of their relative positions and their increasing or diminishing chances of winning. Those who still might win dig deep into their reserves, fighting the pains of exertion, pushing their bodies as far as they physically can, trying to find that last quantum of energy that could see them catch the leader; hoping that the leader does not herself have one last burst in her. Each athlete has a sense of herself but also a sense of the other: the other that stands in her way to victory.

Competition requires an othering, which is why it is inappropriate in many contexts outside of sport. There are team sports, of course, which depend on cooperation and collaboration within the team. But they, of course, also require the othering of an opposition. If we take football, as a very different kind of sport from a 100-metre race, the contrast is not only that one is a team event and the other not, but also that the aim is not just to do your best but also to stop the opponents doing their best. You cannot directly stop opponents performing their best in a race, for instance by cutting into their lane to block them. Indirectly, you might try psychologically to unnerve them beforehand or during the race, but there are even conventional limits to this. In football, however, and many other sports, one's task is in large part to directly stop your opponent, who is, of course, trying to do the same to you. Some sports are turn-taking, such as golf, where each opponent is allocated a time to exercise their abilities. Other sports, like running in lanes, involve the competitors manifesting their abilities simultaneously. Football is one of those oppositional sports in which your aim is not only to manifest your own abilities but, at the same time, to stop your opponents from manifesting theirs. Hence, there is a very direct consciousness of the other in sports of this third kind. After all, while you could meaningfully practice a round of golf or a 100-metre race on your own (though, I'd still say, without ever reproducing an adequate competitive situation), you cannot even play football without an opposition. All you would have is a kick-around or skills practice; and that is not a game of football. It is worth noting, however, that these different kinds of sport do not have entirely strict boundaries. Track races over longer distances do not require lanes and thus while in theory they are about each athlete manifesting their abilities simultaneously, it is also possible to legally prevent an opponent from doing so, for instance, by holding the curve so that an opponent attempting to pass has to go wider and thus run farther.

This engagement between self and other is a basis for competition but, alone, it is not competition quite yet. We must also consider the nature of that engagement. Most obviously, it is one of conflict and opposition. Competition creates the possibility of winners and losers, victory and defeat, in which one is competing *for* something: a trophy, a cash reward or just the honour of victory itself. There is a sense in which competition can require a cooperation, especially in sporting instances. This is because competition often rests upon a codified framework. We can only compete if we agree in what respect we compete, consenting to do so only within certain rules. Hence, the 100-metre race is first of all an agreement on what is to be achieved: getting to the finishing line first, or what some philosophers call the pre-lusory (pre-game-playing) goal. One is not simply competing *simpliciter*, which could take many varied forms. One athlete might seek to look better than all the others, for instance, but this is not what they agreed to compete over. And the competition is not simply a matter of getting to the finishing line first. There are many ways in which one could do that without properly racing; for instance, by throwing nails into the path of your opponents as you run, or riding a bike down the track. The agreement is that one gets to the finishing line by particular means: all starting at the same time and running freely, unimpeded. This agreed method of attaining the prelusory goal is what some philosophers call the lusory (or game-playing) goal. Participants must do this in order for the competition to be possible. Similarly in football, cooperation is required for a game to occur: teams must turn up at the same time, one side must let another kick off, opponents must be allowed to take throw-ins and free kicks, and so on. We cannot have one player holding down the arms of another who wants to take a throw-in, for instance, or a side fielding ten additional players, or going home as soon as they concede a goal.

We need cooperation for a competition to occur, then, but we should not be misled by this into thinking of competition as primarily a cooperative engagement. There is some cooperation, but it is for the sake of competition. We agree a framework so that we can compete. Within that framework, our abilities are pitted against each other, where weaknesses can be exploited, where the stronger can display their dominance over the weaker, and where a winner is perfectly entitled to enjoy their superiority, if they can display it. Victory is the agreed goal, within which framework it is regarded as a major offence if one does not really try. In not trying to win, one is not really playing the game since one is not competing. Indeed, it can be seen as insulting to one's opponents to not try one's best since it is then offering a very different kind of engagement from the one seemingly agreed.

It can help us understand a competitive engagement better if we look at instances outside of sport, of which there are many. We do not want an understanding of competition that applies only to sport since we are looking at competition to better understand the nature of sport rather than vice versa. We see that there are competitions for many different kinds of goal: for resources (between countries), for promotion (between colleagues), for someone's favour (between love rivals). Such competitions can be codified, like sport, but not always. A promotions process should follow defined processes according to stated criteria, as should a dance competition or the competition to be number one in a pop music singles chart (for which the criteria have changed radically over time). Some less codified cases involve tacit or conventional understandings of the 'rules', such as in a competition for the romantic affection of others. Here, part of the challenge is to understand what those rules might be and also finding someone who agrees with your understanding. Does one win their affection by writing the best poetry, for instance, or demonstrating one's physical strength? With dating websites, romantic engagement looks even more explicitly like a competition since in minutes those interested can flick through hundreds of potential partners whose job it is to make the strongest appeal to the viewer. It also seems, however, that some instances of competitive engagement are completely uncodified. Countries might compete for resources, for instance, and to an extent that occurs within a framework of trade agreements. But suppose that the trade agreements break down. The competition can become fierce and chaotic, with no clear framework or terms. Even in the case of wars there have been attempts to create some rules of engagement, such as the Geneva Convention and bans on the use of chemical weapons, but these can break down as wars become more savage. Or consider a street fight in which there are no rules at all. As in war, the opponents might not even know what they are trying to achieve since it is not defined in code nor agreed by the participants.

We can see competition as an oppositional engagement, therefore. There might be some cognate notions, such as that of a contest. Competitions and contests will overlap to a large extent, but if there is to be a distinction it is probably that the latter is *over* something; that is, there is something that is contested. It might be ownership of an object, custody of a pet after a divorce, or the heart of another person, which is contested by multiple parties. Given that it might also simply be a title, such as world champion, then we see how contest and competition can effectively become one, since opponents will compete for what is contested.

Competitiveness

It is clear from this analysis that competition can, in the wrong context, be a distasteful thing. Some people have few competitive urges and might, as a consequence, have no great enthusiasm for sports. There are others, however, who welcome competition gladly, will seek it out at any opportunity, and will be determined to win. These people might find that their competitiveness pervades all aspects of their lives. They try to outpace a stranger on a walk, missing out on the scenery, get the largest slice of cake when they are not particularly hungry, or become upset when they lose a game of tiddlywinks against a child. Competitive people tend to hate losing, even though it is a necessary consequence of there being competition. Still it does not dissuade them from competition, ignoring the fact that almost all competitions will produce more losers than winners. One might think that they must love winning even more than they hate losing, in order to accept the risks, but the evidence on this looks inconclusive.

Rather than say that some people are naturally more competitive than others, we can offer a more socially embedded account. Even if being competitive is a matter of taste, it is not a *simple* matter of taste. The account above suggests that competition rests on an othering: seeing a sharp divide between one's self and others with contested goals that cannot be shared but instead must be fought over for sole dominion. Our interests are then divergent and a conflict is created. This is the basis of competition. Suppose instead that we refuse such a sharp division between self and others.

I am not of course denying that we have individual autonomy as separate human beings. What I mean by a *refusal to
other* is when one sees cooperation as a scenario in which
there is a collective 'we' of which an individual is an integral
part, where goals can be achieved together – perhaps goals
that no one individual could have attained on their own –
and where the rewards are shared and enjoyed by all. Here,
our interests are the same, rather than in conflict, so there
need not be a difference between us. What benefits me also
benefits you; and it will not benefit me unless it benefits you.
The division between self and other is weakened by this
cooperation. The boundary becomes permeable since your
interests bleed into mine and mine into yours.

However, a second aspect of competitive character is
that, even if it is a matter of taste, it is not necessarily a *personal*
matter of taste. Some would have it that people are just born
either competitive or non-competitive. Another idea, however,
is that competition is socially constructed. In the case of sport,
the social construction is clear since the frameworks within
which sport occurs are themselves created jointly and coopera-
tively, within governing bodies; that is, by social institutions.
The social arrangements of sport, then, successfully ensure an
othering of our fellow humans, depicting them as entirely
distinct from us and having conflicting interests, thereby setting up a competitive engagement in which we feel that we
have to overcome them. Team sports provide an intriguing
hybrid, where a collective cooperates in order to defeat
a collective other. Here we have an othering of rival groups.

Othering is the route to competition and clearly many
social systems have inculcated within us a propensity for this

othering. Our neighbours remain distinct economic rivals, for instance, despite us living in the same community. We must compete with them for employment, for whose children have the best school grades, and over the size of our gardens. Migrants are depicted as alien to us, here to take our jobs rather than assisting us as we jointly create a better functioning society. Some groups are othered to such an extent that even their humanity is called into question, in which case a competition for life itself might be invited, in times of war or refugee crises. Degree of competition, which can become as much as a life-or-death struggle, is dependent on degree of othering, according to this analysis. The more brutally a society wants us to treat a group, the more they must be regarded as distinct from and different from us. The opposite also holds where cooperation depends on us seeing the similarities between all, irrespective of race, religion, gender and sexual orientation. We have the same interests, which are best served by seeing ourselves as part of a larger whole.

It is understandable that there will be some ambivalence towards the very notion of competition, then, since it exhibits an ethic that many of us would find abhorrent when considered in the abstract. Does this mean that competition is then inherently an evil? I will say something on this later, in Chapter 5, but have still more to say here too.

Non-competitive Sport

A well-known option for those who do not like competition is to pursue non-competitive sports. I should acknowledge these not least to show that the connection between sport and competition is itself contested. Hence, some like to run on the street in a non-competitive way, still enjoying their physicality and exercising their abilities but without any stress of winning and losing and nor any requirement of othering an opponent. Sometimes this is a solo activity but it can also be with a companion in a non-competitive way, finding a mutually agreeable pace. Similarly, many like to swim or cycle, sometimes donning full cycling attire to do so.

An issue is whether such forms of activity genuinely count as sport rather than mere recreation, exercise or leisure pursuit. We already have seen in the previous chapter that merely exercising one's physical abilities is not enough for an activity to count as a sport. And nor does it follow automatically that anything that we could do in sport competitively remains sport when it is done non-competitively, as perhaps is the case with running. The issue of othering also plays a role here.

What is the other in mainstream competitive sports is reasonably clear. The others are your competitors: people or teams against whom you are pitted, any of whom is a potential winner and thus someone contesting that title with you. But if sport needs an other, what about non-competitive sports? A possible answer is that non-competitive sport involves what we might call competing against oneself. For example, one knows one's previous best time on a cycle route and may try to beat that, which duplicates a cycling time trial where cyclists compete against each other by taking turns to ride the same route individually with staggered departures. In this case, one is not trying to beat another person but an earlier version of yourself. Similarly, many now use running apps with GPS to track and record the route, logging best times. We can still understand the sport in terms of othering, therefore, but where the other is the former self and with the 'competitor' treating this former self, artificially, as if it is not her. One adopts the present self as one's real self and other previous selves and their best times as the opponent to be beaten. One does not, in contrast, treat one's former self as one's real self, having a title or time to defend. The latter stance might well be adopted in different circumstances: for instance, if one holds a world record one certainly understands this as an achievement of oneself, even if it is in the distant past, and might be pleased when it endures and others fail to beat it.

Competing against oneself might seem possible, therefore, if one can other some part of oneself to be one's competitor. However, that does not settle the matter since there is another consideration that might carry more weight. In his *Philosophical Investigations*, Wittgenstein argued against the possibility of an individual having a private language, where this meant a language spoken by that one individual alone. The reason was that when the individual used a term – call it S – they could not be sure that they were using S correctly or only thinking that they use it correctly. Why does this not happen with ordinary, natural languages? The answer is that these are not private. They are spoken by many people, who can correct each other if words are misused. Meanings are normative in that words have a proper meaning and it can only be other language users who correct us if we get a meaning wrong.

The application of a private language-style argument to the notion of competing against oneself is relatively straightforward. A single individual cannot alone determine whether or not she has followed the rules so as to allow a secure judgement of victory or defeat since she might misremember the criteria by which victory is to be judged, she might bend the rules in her favour, or she might just decide on an entirely new set of rules during the engagement. For example, on a bicycle machine (with an electronic readout), someone might try to beat their record distance for a twenty-minute ride. If they are falling behind schedule at the fifteen-minute mark, however, there is nothing to stop them turning the bike down to an easier setting or deciding to beat the record for a thirty-minute ride instead, or just deciding that the attempt did not count. The point is, as outlined above, that competition usually occurs within a codified framework that determines the terms of the contest and permits a definitive decision regarding its winners and losers. In non-competitive sports there is no such codification other than what the individual decides, who then has the freedom to change their decision. In competitive sports, the codification comes from an authority other than a participant.

What, though, of cases of competition where the codification has broken down, like wars and street fights where 'anything goes'? Mixed martial arts (MMA) is a bit like this. Doesn't this show that codification is not always needed? What seems really to count is that there is an other, against whom you can compete, and we said in these cases that an earlier self could fill the role of other. A war is certainly a competition of sorts, if that doesn't trivialise it too much, and I grant that it can be uncodified. So can't, then, a non-competitive sport be uncodified? The problem is, however, that the analogy starts to break down. It is not always clear who won a war and it is not unknown for it to end and both sides to claim victory, or a seeming victory to be later understood as defeat by historians. Competition in sport is supposed to have clear verdicts. This includes cases of a draw, where the result is tied; but even then there is a clear verdict that it is a tie. Such indisputable verdicts can only occur within a codified framework, which we cannot have in this case because of the lack of an outside authority. There can be no distinction drawn between someone really winning against themselves and only thinking that they have won against themselves. Even MMA has a definitive verdict, declared by a non-contestant.

Where this leads us, then, is to doubt that non-competitive sports are really competitive at all. It gives us scepticism about a notion of competing against oneself. We looked at that possibility potentially to defeat the view that non-competitive sports are just recreation or ways of taking exercise and thus not truly sport after all. Wearing the latest cycling fashion is not on its own sufficient to make a cycle ride sport, of course. We need a more substantial marker than that. And nor is the exercise of our physical capacities enough, as we do that when we dance or screw in a light bulb. They are not sport either. So what we have is some form of non-competitive physical activity that people call non-competitive sport. Given the want of a substantial reason why these activities are sport, then, we should remain sceptical about the category of non-competitive sports. There are plenty of perfectly healthy and worthy physical activities that are not sport and we can add so-called non-competitive sports to them. In doing so, we preserve the connection between competition and sport. Sport is competitive.

Harmless Competition

We have seen, then, that there are potentially undesirable, unseemly or downright destructive aspects to competition. Suppose I nudge someone out of the way and beat them to the last seat on the bus. I have contested something and won it. Does that make me a better person? Should I be proud of my actions? Would I be right to celebrate my success? Again, should the participant be pleased to have fought a war, whether they have won or not? Competition, in the abstract, does not seem necessarily a good thing and has great potential to be a bad thing since it requires othering and selfish goals.

In spite of this, might it be possible to create a space for competition that is harmless, or possibly even capable of delivering good? This, I suggest, is one thing that sport aims to do. It aims to create a safe space or bubble in which competition can occur, protected by its codes, and, in so doing, allows us to freely develop our capacities and hence to flourish and grow.

These are some grand claims that, accordingly, require a justification. A key component of such a justification is that sport is a safe space for competition because it involves competition for competition's sake. In the case of war, two countries might be competing for a resource, where the winner gains something and the loser ends up worse off than they were before. In competing for a promotion, someone gets a salary increase and the others don't. In an economic competition of nations, the loser often faces negative health consequences, ruin or poverty. And if we had to compete for life-saving drugs, it would be perverse to enjoy the competitive aspect of that.

What is distinctive about the sporting case, in contrast, is that the goals – the prelusory or pre-game-playing goals – do not matter. They are inconsequential. They are not matters of life and death or even of serious detriment. Hence, in high jump, it is not as if anything major hinges on getting to the other side of the bar. The losers do not die so that the winner can live. One aims to get over the bar, but only for the sake of getting over the bar. Similarly, whoever arrives first at the finish of a swim is entirely inconsequential as far as the universe is concerned. Of course, the winner gets a prize, and in professional sports there are riches to be won, but these are entirely decided by us because we want to reward winners to incentivise maximum effort all round. The rewards are entirely our construction. Contrast that to a real 'competition' that two swimmers might have in trying to escape a crocodile. As the old joke has it, you can't outswim a crocodile but you can outswim your companion, and in this instance the loser gets eaten. More than prize money rests on this outcome. The 'winner' might be relieved at the result. I doubt that her feelings would be describable as happiness. The main point, however, is that during the swim itself it would be perverse of either swimmer to be enjoying competing against the other. In swimming in a sporting context, however, that is perfectly possible. You can enjoy the act of swimming but enjoy it even more because you are doing so competitively. Such arguments extend easily to other sports. Nothing really hinges on footballs going into nets or golf balls into holes, nothing important is determined by the length of someone's jump, whereas it could if someone had to jump for their life. And nothing important rests on balancing on a beam, though it might in other circumstances.

Given the unimportant goals, then, we are at liberty to enjoy the competition, knowing that our opponents remain unharmed even if we beat them. Of course, they might be sad if they lose, but this is because they have lost, not because they therefore suffer material damage, and they have already consented to the possibility of defeat in entering into the competition. This is one way in which it is important that sport respects the agency and autonomy of its participants. We must enter the competition freely, knowing that defeat is possible. It would not really be sport if, for instance, a participant had been forced to take part or if they were doing so under personal threat in the event of defeat. It is assumed that athletes compete because they want to compete and accept the incentive of victory as an ample reason to risk the defeat. None of this is to deny that the ideal I am describing is often disappointed. There is abuse in sport as it is practised, which often involves athletes being entirely trapped within a system. And there is physical and sexual abuse of athletes too. When I speak of sport as a safe space, I do not mean safe in absolute terms but only as a safe space for competition in the sense described above: where competition is for the sake of competition, where the participants want to compete.

There are various reasons why someone might want to compete, such as for fame or riches. However, here is a more reflective reason for wanting to compete; one that I believe is a real motivation for many participants in sport. The goal of victory and the harmlessness of the competition allows us to develop our physical capacities beyond a point they would reach otherwise. For example, would any human ever have run 100 metres in ten seconds without sport? That is doubtful. There are certainly occasions in life when running fast is an advantage, and some might even enjoy running as a daily recreation and get faster as a result of it. I am suggesting more than that, though. Competition creates an additional incentive, with the possibility of victory, that drives us far beyond a point we would have reached without it. The contest provides a rational basis for the hours, weeks and years of dedication that are required to take performance levels to their highest. Even those who engage only in amateur sports will see that competition raises their performance levels. It pushes them to persist through the pain that can be felt in maximal exercise of their powers, to push themselves to their limits and not to give up as soon as they find it hard.

Cheating

Sometimes, the incentive of victory can have a negative effect, however, where some are prepared to win at all costs. It is possible to be too competitive, taking the desire for victory beyond what is fair to one's opponents. In egregious cases, this can tip over into cheating.

We noted how sports occur within a codified framework. Usually this is in the form of rules or laws of the relevant sport. There are cases, such as cricket, which historically have also encouraged an informal ethos or tradition in which the game should be played in a certain spirit, supposedly of respect, honour and honesty. The power of this informal ethos might be eroded through time, but it illustrates the point that the codification of a sport can be either formal or informal and cultural. I explained above about the significance of this codification. It allows the competition to be structured, and for it to be within a shared set of parameters. It is clear what it is to win, how victory can and cannot be achieved, and so on.

The competition into which we freely enter is one in which it is permissible to seek every advantage within the rules. This is not considered incorrect or unfair at all. So in boxing, for example, the fighters are allowed to weigh as much as they like up to a prescribed limit for their weight category, and it is not considered unsporting of them to get as close as possible to this limit without exceeding it. Generally, it is accepted that competitors may try everything they can within and up to the prescribed limits that will give them an advantage.

Where the matter of cheating is determined by a place on a sliding scale, up to a permissible limit, cheating is nevertheless considered to be an all or nothing matter and morally reprehensible when it occurs. Hence, exceeding a limit by a little gets treated the same as exceeding it by a lot. This happens, for example, when an athlete exceeds a permissible level of a banned substance in their body. Why it is so condemned, if one is to seek a justification, is that it breaks the informal contract into which athletes entered when they agreed to compete. The aim is to complete a defined task in a certain way, called the lusory (game playing) goal. For example: to get to the other side of the bar by jumping over it, to score a goal in a certain way without using your hands, to get the small ball into a hole in the ground using a stick rather than by carrying it there, and so on. In agreeing to play, one agrees to the prescriptions and proscriptions of the codification since, otherwise, one is not really playing the sport. Thus, if I 'beat' my opponent at 'tennis' after having drugged him with a performance-lowering drug, have I really won a game of tennis? If I sabotage my opponent's car the night before a Formula 1 race, have I really beaten them when their car subsequently runs much slower than mine? The rules can be seen as constituting the sport such that, if I cease to follow them, I cease to play the sport and thus any apparent victory I win is only illusory. If I walk under the bar, to get to the other side, instead of jumping over it, I have not really competed at high jump. It is hard to see how anyone could be satisfied with such a 'victory', even if they succeed in an undetected deception. One assumes the temptation resides in what surrounds the victory – the fame and adulation – rather than the victory itself, which can be no more than pyrrhic.

Even in the case of cheating, however, we find it necessary to introduce some nuance into an account. Cheating is not simply a matter of breaking the rules of the sport since some sports permit frequent infringements of their rules where these are not deemed to be cheating. In rugby and football, for example, and many other sports, infringements can be committed but where one accepts a penalty for doing so. We can call these compensable infringements. In football, it is not considered cheating to foul an opponent since the penalty for the foul compensates the opponent, as part of the sport's codification. Certain close contact oppositional sports will almost inevitably produce such fouls so it is not as if we can simply instruct the players not to commit them. This is not so much of an issue in turn-taking sports, such as pole vault, where foul jumps can simply be excluded. But in oppositional contact sports the only realistic response is to accept that infringements occur and codify the penalties. This almost always works well, though there can be controversies. There are egregious infringements, such as when Luis Suárez handled the ball to stop a certain goal in the last minute of a World Cup quarter-final for Uruguay against Ghana in 2006, which was widely considered cheating despite the concession of the penalty (which was missed). Presumably, this was considered cheating because the penalty did not compensate for what the foul had taken away. There could also be cases when a type of infringement is not anticipated and the penalty is not known, as when VfB Stuttgart accidentally played too many non-national players versus Leeds United, against the rules at the time, through a mix-up over substitutions that the match officials mistakenly permitted. The authorities had to make an ad hoc decision over the penalty for the offence. It is also possible, of course, that the officials abolish a type of compensable infringement, as in the case of false starts in sprint races. Competitors were allowed one false start until the suspicion became too great that some were exploiting the possibility by trying to go too early and gain an advantage. Now, any false start means disqualification.

We have explored a range of issues around competition. We have seen that, while not all competition is sport, there are some good reasons to accept that all sport is competitive. Furthermore, we can consider sport to be a safe space for competition since it is competition for the sake of competition. If one plays sport for the competition, this makes cheating something of a puzzle, since the cheat effectively opts out of the competition and seeks only the appearance of victory by some other means.

3   Definition

Understanding Definition

We have looked at physicality and we have looked at competition. These are key aspects of sport and likely to be vital components in any theory of sport. What we do not yet have, however, is a definition of sport. Dancing is both physical and competitive but it is not sport. Why not? To answer that, we will need to know what sport is.

It somewhat goes against the spirit of philosophy to be this far into our enquiry but to not yet have defined our subject matter. There was a time when the first thing a trainee philosopher was told was to define their terms. Here, as with other subjects, things are not quite so simple, however. Some bright student one day responded with 'define define' and the whole project of starting with definitions was scuppered. It turns out that definition is itself not easy to define and, when we ask for a definition, it could mean many different things. A further complication is that what counts as a definition for sport might not be the same as the definition for horse or electron or person. There could be different types of definition. Nevertheless, the point stands that if we want to know whether this or that activity is sport or not, and understand why it is sport or not, this has to be with reference to some concept of sport and understanding of what sport itself is.

One project would be to offer necessary and sufficient conditions for something being a sport. The search for necessary and sufficient conditions is connected with the idea that the thing in question has a nature or essence. For example, we can say that something is a circle if it is a one-sided two-dimensional figure where every point on the extremity of the figure is equidistant from the centre. This is necessary and sufficient for anything to be a circle in that, first, the condition must be met to be a circle and, second, if anything meets this condition then it must be a circle. This allows us to say that the definition provides the nature or essence of a circle. It tells us what it is to be a circle. Similarly, we might say that there is an essence to a triangle, which mathematicians know, an essence to an electron, which physicists know, and an essence to a chromosome, which biologists know.

A problem with this approach, however, is that it is not clear that everything has such an essence. It is relatively straightforward to provide the essence for being a circle since this is a simple geometrical object, as first defined by Euclid, and where all instances will have a respect in which they are identical. Not all circles are identical in every respect since they can vary by size. But they are all identical in their circularity, by which we mean that they all satisfy the above definition. Circles have relatively few properties and relatively few variances, and the same is true of electrons. Can such an approach be taken with far more complicated phenomena, though? Biological essentialism is controversial, such as whether species have essences. Sport is an even more complicated matter than that, since it permits all manner of variety.

Is there anything in common to ice dance, field hockey, e-sports, MMA and pole vault that makes them all sports?

Wittgenstein's Challenge

In a famous sequence in his *Philosophical Investigations* (sections 65–71), Wittgenstein compared languages with games and argued that there is no single definition satisfying either concept. The passages have spawned many interpretations and what I say here is not a contribution to that scholarship. I raise Wittgenstein's view for two reasons. First, we can take from it the point that not everything has a definition. There is no essence to language, he says, just as there is no essence to games, and necessary and sufficient conditions cannot be supplied for them. If this is right, it suggests a crisis for the project of philosophical analysis because it will mean that necessary and sufficient conditions do not exist for every phenomenon. Second, however, the example used as a concept for which there can be no definition is game. Games hold an important relation to sport, as we shall see, so the claim that game cannot be defined might be more than a convenient example for us, if we are interested in sport.

Just in case the idea that game and language are indefinable is a troubling one, Wittgenstein did offer more than a negative thesis. After all, we speak about games and language and we seem able to communicate when we do so. It seems that we must mean something when we use the word 'game', then, but how can we do so if it has no single definition? In place of that, Wittgenstein argued that game was a family resemblance concept. If one looks at the various children of a large biological family, one can see a series of resemblances. Three of them might have the same sort of nose but another one doesn't. The odd one out has a similar eyes to another, though, and the same curly hair as three siblings. Some but not all are similar in height, face shape, eyebrows, and so on. It might be that there isn't one single feature that they all have in common; hence, there is no necessary condition for being a member of this family. Some of the features the family members have in common are shared with other people who are not members of this family, so no feature is a sufficient condition for family membership. Nevertheless, we can tell from the overall resemblance who is a member of the family and who is not.

Wittgenstein thought that this is what we would have to say in the case of games. Some games involve balls but some do not. Some involve direct opposition but some do not. Some involve running but some do not. Some have winners but some do not (like ring a ring o' roses). Some involve vigorous physical activity but some do not (like chess). There are no necessary and sufficient conditions for games, but we are able to use the concept nevertheless because of a family resemblance among all the things that are games. Family resemblance is thus good enough to make a concept usably coherent.

Suppose, then, that Wittgenstein is right and there are some concepts for which there are no necessary and sufficient conditions. Suppose sport were one such concept. Where does that leave philosophy? Is there anything we might still do in order to understand sport better philosophically?

One option is that philosophy can give a theory of something even though it cannot give an analysis of it. For example, we might not be able to analyse what goodness is (some say 'the good'). Perhaps goodness is entirely basic and there is nothing more fundamental than it in terms of which we can understand goodness if we do not already. Nevertheless, we might still be able to say coherent things about goodness. We could say what role it plays in our moral thinking and our actions, for instance, and how it connects with related concepts such as rightness. We could say what sort of thing goodness is and where it comes from: the questions dealt with in meta-ethics. This would leave us with a theory of goodness even if it is not a philosophical analysis of more basic notions.

The comparison with meta-ethics suggests another option for the case of sport. Analogous to meta-ethics for the realm of the good would be what we can call the ontology of sport. Here our task is to look at what sort of things constitute sport. Is it the rules? The activities? Or would the explanation of sport also have to invoke other kinds of entities, such as social institutions? I believe so. What I will present in the remainder of this chapter can be understood as a non-essentialist theory in the ontology of sport. I will describe some of the key features of sport but without offering a definition in the analytic sense. There will be no necessary and sufficient conditions but there will be an account and it should still be informative.

Games

We cannot, however, leave the subject of games just yet. I have said that games and sport are not the same thing but the significance of games to sport should be acknowledged. A greater understanding of games will take us some of the way to understanding sport even if they are not exactly the same thing (and, after all, they are called the Olympic *Games* so clearly the connection is close enough that the difference doesn't matter in every context).

We saw how Wittgenstein thought that game could not be defined and we had to accept that it was a family resemblance concept instead. We have yet to decide whether this conclusion is secure. What proof did Wittgenstein offer? When we look at the text we see that there is very little by way of argument. There is only a series of diverse examples followed by a swift pronouncement that they have nothing significant in common. Of course, games were not Wittgenstein's primary concern. Language was. But if he was using the example of games to illuminate a feature of language then he ought to be right about games.

Bernard Suits in *The Grasshopper*, a key book in the philosophy of sport, argues that Wittgenstein was wrong about games. His conclusion that game is indefinable is hasty. Effectively, Wittgenstein should have looked harder for something in common to all games. There are likely to be many cases where diverse things have little or nothing in common at a low level of description but have something significant in common at a higher level of abstraction. For example, Abraham Lincoln had little in common with a worm but it would be too hasty to say that they had absolutely nothing significant in common. They both belonged to the group of living creatures. It's easy to find differences between card games, ball games, running games and ring a ring o' roses but that doesn't mean that there is nothing interesting that they have in common at a more abstract level.

Duly, Suits offers a definition of game that he thinks answers the challenge Wittgenstein posed. He also thinks that the definition is not that difficult to discover or understand. He says:

> To play a game is to attempt to achieve a specific state of affairs (prelusory goal), using only means permitted by rules (lusory means), where the rules prohibit use of more efficient in favour of less efficient means (constitutive rules), and where the rules are accepted just because they make possible such an activity (lusory attitude). I also offer the following simpler and, so to speak, more portable version of the above: playing a game is the voluntary attempt to overcome unnecessary obstacles. (*The Grasshopper*, pp. 54–5)

The idea of a game as a voluntary attempt to overcome unnecessary obstacles is simplicity itself. Even in the more extended definition, the only remotely technical terms employed are lusory and prelusory and they are there just to assist us. They are not strictly part of the definition on pain of circularity since lusory means game playing (from the Greek *ludos* = game).

Let us consider some examples and how they fit with Suits's definition. This will help us to understand the definition better.

We can start with a simple board game: Monopoly, since it is so well known. The point is to win all the money and put the other players out of business. This is the specific state of affairs one aims to achieve. But the rules tell you that you have to do it in a very particular and rather elaborate way, throwing the dice, moving round the board, buying property, constructing houses and so on. All sorts of unnecessary obstacles are put in your way. You might have to go to jail if you land on a certain square and there are Chance and Community Chest cards, a lot of which are forfeits. You also have to pay rent if you land on an opponent's property. Others can stop you doing what you want to do since they are aiming for the same goal as you – buying Mayfair before you get there, for instance. We accept all these rules because doing so is what allows the playing of Monopoly to be possible. Without those rules, it wouldn't be Monopoly.

Now let us move on to a less formalised game: ring a ring o' roses. I choose this example as it's the sort of case Wittgenstein introduced to show how diverse games could be. We might not think of this as a game because it is so informal, but there is good reason to think it so nevertheless. It is both a singing and a dancing game, usually where one holds hands with others in a rotating circle singing a particular song, on the last line of which you all jump to the floor as fast as you can. We perform this ritualised and choreographed song and dance purely for the fun of it, and to play we have to follow the informal rules. We thus adopt a lusory, game-playing attitude to the activity. If someone refused to jump down at the end, they would have stopped playing the game. And performing the actions has no point other than playing the game.

As a third example of a game, consider repeatedly bouncing a ball against a wall and catching it. This is about as informal a game as you can get. It is still a game nevertheless. There are no winners and losers. There are no opponents. But it is a game nevertheless. If one desires the state of having the ball in one's hand, the easiest thing would be to never let it go. Throwing it against a wall, judging the flight of its return and then catching it is effectively an unnecessary obstacle.

How could this definition of game be applied to the case of sport? Again, I have not yet said how I take sport to differ from games, but it is interesting to see whether Suits's definition of game also fits a regular case of sport. We find that it can fit perfectly. In pole vault, for example, the specific state of affairs to be achieved is to get to the other side of the bar without knocking it off. However, there are rules about how one does so. The most efficient way would probably be to walk under the bar. As long as you don't crash into the vertical supports, there is very little chance of disturbing the bar that way. Nevertheless, the rules favour a less efficient means of achieving this state. You have to jump over the bar instead of walking under it. Why would anyone put themselves to the trouble of getting over such a high bar when they could easily walk under it? They do so because it enables them to play the game. It allows a game to be made of it, competing against others. It is the adoption of a lusory attitude to the end state of affairs.

I will not multiply the sporting examples beyond necessity since there are other issues to which we should turn. There does not seem to be anything particularly special about the example of pole vault, however. One does not struggle to identify prelusory goals, lusory means and constitutive rules for other sports, as with football, volleyball, the beam exercise in gymnastics, the hammer, high diving and so on.

All this does is see us return to our starting point, however. Even though Suits's account of games fits also with sports, it is still the case that some activities are clearly games (poker, Monopoly, ring a ring o' roses) and others are clearly sports (boxing, handball, high hurdles). We still want to know why.

How good a theory of games and/or sport has Suits given us? I accept that it is adequate for most of our purposes. One could quibble over details, of course. He has defined what it is to play a game rather than defined game itself. We ought to have the capacity to adapt his words so that they concern games rather than game playing, however (for example, 'a game is something that is played when . . .'). Nor is it true that, in every game, every less efficient means of achieving the goal is favoured over more efficient means. Usually games offer some constraints on what means can be employed but they don't constrain every efficient means. In the game of catching a ball, for instance, one doesn't have to do it blindfolded. And in pole vault, they do allow you a long, bendy pole to get over the high bar, which is more efficient than having no pole at all or one that cannot bend. But these are only quibbles, and I am happy to move on to sport accepting the spirit of Suits's account of games.

The Institutional Theory

I will offer an account in which all sports are to be understood as games but where being a sport requires some additional mark that not all games will have. Hence, football clearly has this mark but the card game of snap does not. In some cases, such as chess, it is not entirely clear whether or not it has the extra mark. It will be another virtue of the account, however, that it is able to explain how some activities can have an uncertain or disputed status. Finally, I will go on to examine a case where the status of a particular activity is right now under debate and where it is open how that debate will conclude. Again, the account I offer explains how this is a possibility.

What, then, is required in addition to being a game for something to be a sport? Is there some distinct additional feature? If we look for it, it is hard to find. For example, one might be encouraged by the fact that not all games involve the exercise of a physical skill whereas all sports do and then venture that sports must include physical skills. A game of twenty questions to guess who I am, for instance, requires no physical skill. This suggestion runs aground, though, since there are plenty of games that involve physical skills without being sports, such as playing catch with a ball. What about saying, alternatively, that all sports decide on winners and losers whereas not all games do. A game of catch has no winner. Again, though, there are plenty of games that have winners so this does not seem to be what divides sport from games either.

One could continue looking for such features and others are welcome to explore those possibilities. Instead, however, I offer a different kind of theory: an anti-essentialist one. Sport, I suggest, is a status bestowed upon some forms of practice by certain historically evolved social institutions. There is no essential difference between games and sport since those relevant social institutions have the power to determine what is sport, by bestowing that status upon a form of practice. An important point here is that the institutions empowered to bestow the status of sport are not doing so with reference to some pre-existing essence of sport since there is nothing that makes something sport other than their own verdicts. This is a point about direction of fit, which seems best illustrated by analogy with the contents of a shopping basket. In the first case, I could look into someone's shopping basket and make a list of the contents. If I do so accurately, I obtain a list that matches what is there. In a second case, however, concerning my own basket, I made a list first, and as I was shopping I put in my basket all and only what was on the list. Again, I get a basket and a list that correspond. But there is a vital difference between these two cases of correspondence. In the first one, the contents of the basket determine the list and in the second case the list determines the contents of the basket. The institutional theory of sport tells us that the status of sport is determined in the second kind of way. The relevant institutions, about which I will say more shortly, decide what counts as sport. They are not merely reporting what is sport after having identified salient features of the activity in question. This is not to deny that the institutional verdicts on what to deem sport can be guided by historical precedent with what has been deemed sport before. It is, however, such historical matters that guide the application of the title of sport, rather than a predetermined essence of sport.

A motivation for an institutional theory of sport is the observation, perhaps too obvious to record, that sport is a social phenomenon. We have already seen one way in which it is. Sport requires an opponent against whom there is a competitive interaction (which itself is to be explained in an institutional theory). This requires an engagement between self and other and is social in this sense. There is, however, a more important way in which sport is a social phenomenon. Sport involves various forms of practice situated within a set of complex social structures that are responsible for the creation and enforcement of its codification. A game of football is bigger than the ninety minutes played between twenty-two people. It is a socially situated practice in which many parties have a stake: the governing bodies, the supporters, the sponsors, the media companies. It is the product of historically evolved and negotiated norms: its rules, presentation, customs, conventions and ethos. These structures produce a set of institutions with the capacity to bestow the status of sport upon certain forms of practice. The institutions are the gatekeepers that bestow the honorific title of sport on a type of activity and enforce its compliance with the required norms, ensuring that the activity remains a sporting one.

What are these social institutions, which are the key component of the institutional theory? They can take many forms. There are some entities that are clearly and explicitly institutions, such as the governing bodies of each sport and those with an overarching purview of all sport, such as the IOC (International Olympic Committee) and WADA (World Anti-Doping Agency). These institutions might form a hierarchical structure both in terms of having national bodies under them and bodies representing different sports. But some of the relevant institutions are less formal in organisation while still representing an important and powerful interest. Media companies and advertising agencies will be examples of this kind. One might think that these are far less influential in sport than the governing bodies, but that is often a matter of the relative power structures of the competing interests. Advertising interests can change the way a sport looks, for example, and even the format of the sport. Consider how American sports have so many breaks in play so that advertising can occur. Other powerful interests will include players' agents, sports clubs and even influences that seem superficially to be outside of sport, such as political interests, but which nevertheless are a part of the complex ecosystem in which sport is sustained. Governments often fund sport, for instance.

One could draw a comparison with the art world and how it bestows the status of art upon certain forms of practice. Painting is art, for example, but basket weaving is only craft. The art world was challenged by innovative work such as Marcel Duchamp's *Fountain*, Carl Andre's *Equivalent VIII* and Tracey Emin's *My Bed*, but accepted them all as art, agreeing that they be displayed in galleries.

This raises an issue, however. If we are to reject essentialism about sport and, as I would be happy to do, essentialism about art, then what makes the institutions of art different from the institutions of sport? There is no point saying that one deals with art and the other deals with sport since we are using these institutions to elucidate what it is to be art and what it is to be sport. The answer has to be in other terms, therefore, and I suggest that we just say that these two worlds – these two large clusters of institutions – evolved from different starting points, followed different historical paths, and have brought us to separate places too. The institutions of art grew around certain practices, originally restricted to painting, sculpture, music and so on, and came to play a role in shaping the development of those practices. Further, they decided what new practices could be added under the same umbrella, such as performance art. The institutions of sport grew out of other activities, such as running, jumping, throwing and swimming. They too have historically evolved and bestowed an honorific title on a range of additional practices, such as mountain biking and synchronised swimming. This evolution is not complete as new sports can still be added, such as esports. It is a corollary of such an institutional theory that the concept of sport, like the concept of art, is a relatively recent invention, arriving in our culture as those relevant institutions developed. Specific activities of running and painting existed before anyone deemed them sport and art.

How is the status of sport bestowed on a practice? An institutional theory need not say that there is any formal process by which a game is elevated to the status of sport. The historical reality will be messy, often involving a negotiation between competing powers. Clearly, some bodies are more powerful than others. Acceptance into the Olympics by the IOC bestows a status that other sporting institutions would find hard to overturn. It is the most validating honorific. But achievement of that status usually comes after a period of negotiations among other interests. There are likely to be internal disputes over codification and proper authority within a sport, petitioning and negotiation through a number of iterations before a non-sport becomes a sport. This process is itself a complex social interaction.

I have said that sport is consequently a normative concept. Those norms are themselves the result of a negotiation within the sporting institutions and could continue to be disputed and evolve.

The fact that sports have to have winners and losers, or at least clear verdicts, is the outcome of such a norm. Games of catch and ring a ring o' roses have no clear winner. Note that Suits's definition of game makes no mention of winners. If those games wanted to have the status of sport, it is almost certain that they would need to provide rules that delivered conclusive victory and defeat to satisfy this norm. The norm of victory need not be stated explicitly but could nevertheless be significant in how the institutions of sport view a candidate sport and regard it as fit to be welcomed under their umbrella.

Sports also have an important physical component, where a bodily capacity has to be exercised. We can get this in games too, of course, so it is not sufficient to make something sport. It might be enough for an activity not to be accepted as sport, though, if it is deemed to lack the requisite physicality. Chess is an obvious example of a highly competitive and codified game that is not usually accepted as a sport. This is debated, it must be said, with some reporting how physically strenuous it is to think as hard as some of the best chess players must and how fit they need to be to do so. We might be sceptical about the status of esports since video games could be considered more like chess than football. Esports do have a significant physical dimension, however, since success depends on being adept with the controls. Moment #37 is famous in Street Fighter 2, for instance, because its execution required virtually frame-perfect inputs, which very few players had the dexterity to perform.

Another norm is that the sport be regimented and codified. Of course, this is not sufficient to make something a sport since the rules of knockout whist, a card game, are as codified as many sports. The norm is real, however, even if it operates as a *sine qua non*. A big challenge games sometimes have in attaining the status of sport is codification, especially if they do not have a clear governance structure capable of implementing a single code. It is also possible, on this account, that the status of sport be withdrawn from an activity if it contravenes the norms adopted by the relevant institutions. Various forms of hunting provide a good example of this, in those cases where animals are killed. These may have been thought of as sports in the past, and perhaps still are in the country that is always the great exception, the United States. (I was pretty shocked when I visited a sports shop in Texas; it was not what I expected at all.) Mostly, however, we have moved to a norm in which it cannot be sport if it involves deliberate killing of life, although some of the skills used in hunting have been incorporated into harmless sports such as clay pigeon shooting and biathlon.

Given its codified, physical and competitive nature, it might seem a mystery why something like ballroom dancing is not deemed sport. If we were essentialists about sport, we might well say that it really is sport, even though it is rarely recognised as such. We could point to some very similar activities that are sport: ice dance and gymnastic floor exercises, for example. An institutional theory of sport at least offers an explanation of why ballroom is not a sport even though it has these similarities to sport. As a practice, it has been evolved under a different set of organisations from sport. Dance has belonged to the art or entertainment world and under the governance of their institutions. For ballroom to become sport would require a disruptive wrenching away from its traditional home.

The Future of Parkour

I will end this chapter by examining an activity for which the future status looks up for grabs; where even now there are various formal and informal institutions considering whether this could become a sport. Would it need to make changes to become so and would it be willing to make those changes?

I will consider this question in relation to one Associated Press article from late 2018, 'Parkour Eyed for

2024 Olympics by Gymnastics Officials amid Complaints'. I choose this article not because it is the definitive word on the topic – it is just one point of view – but because it perfectly illustrates many of the issues that I have just presented in an abstract way.

Parkour developed over thirty years ago, which still qualifies it as a relatively new activity or recreation. Since then its profile has been raised high enough that most readers will know of it. It is clearly a physically arduous activity requiring high degrees of skill, fitness and daring. That is a good start for any form of practice with ambitions to be a sport. Despite the speed with which it has arrived in popular culture, there is already discussion, as the above article reports, of it becoming an Olympic event. As I have stated, were it to do so it would have received the highest possible validation as a sport.

However, the path to Olympic recognition is a troubled one since there are competing interests in play. There could be a clear route but one that requires coming under the jurisdiction of gymnastics, if the news article is to be believed. There are many prominent voices within parkour that do not want to be subordinated to the International Gymnastics Federation. A spokesperson for Parkour Earth, representing six national associations, thinks of it as a hostile takeover. They want to codify it and monetise it, they say. Indeed, to be recognised as a sport would almost certainly require a high degree of codification. While there are recognised moves deployed in parkour, as a *traceur* traverses the built environment, the activity is formally uncodified at present. There are clear aims and objectives, but parkour is still seen as an expression of freedom amid a potentially oppressive and inhuman environment. Codification could be seen as anathema to that freedom which parkour reasserts, hence the charge that the history and authenticity of parkour would have to be lost for Olympic status to be gained. To become a codified sport would be to open greater commercial potential, certainly; but would the founders of parkour want that?

We see competing interests, therefore, and a political struggle over who has the right to represent the activity in any future negotiation. Football was in a similar position in the mid nineteenth century. There were rival local associations, each with their different codes. Arguably, the biggest advance for that sport was when a single set of laws of the game was adopted, and a good set of laws too that made it an enjoyable game to play and to watch.

One would suspect that the Gymnastics Federation has a pretty good idea of what it would take for parkour to be accepted as an Olympic sport. They understand the rules of that particular game. The question is whether those within parkour would be willing to cooperate with the more sanitised version that would almost certainly emerge. The Olympic version is likely to reduce the risks to participants since they will not want to broadcast injuries on live television or be seen as encouraging recklessness. This again sits uncomfortably with the current practitioners. Olympic parkour would probably occur in a sanitised purpose-built stadium with a series of regulation obstacles and a prescribed route over them, with safety helmets, knee and shoulder pads, and cushioned landings for any who slip. A high level of personal danger violates one of the norms of sport yet seems intrinsic to parkour as it is currently practised.

More than that, there is a philosophical struggle to be had for the soul of parkour. It is anti-establishment: an anti-authoritarian counterculture of freedom from constraint. It is subversive and underground. The very idea of parkour is that the constructions participants traverse were not intended for that purpose. This is the challenge of parkour: for a human to regain mastery of an inhuman landscape. A venue of custom-made obstacles violates parkour's own *raison d'être*, then.

I do not know which way this one will go. Perhaps there will be a sanitised form of parkour at some future Olympics. My point in using the example, however, is to show how the status of sport is a result of a process of debate and negotiation, often only informal and disparate, within a host of social structures. It is a contested and normative matter. Parkour is not yet sport, I would say. Whether it becomes so will depend on changes either within parkour or within the institutions that decide what is sport.

I do not, then, have a definition of sport. The institutional theory says that there is no definition of sport, even if there is a definition of game. Sport is whatever the institutions of sport decide to call sport. This does not mean that their decisions are entirely unconstrained and capricious. Verdicts will be decided on the basis of mostly implicit norms of sport, which have themselves evolved within the development of the sport world. We can thus reject essentialism about sport – it does not have an immutable nature – while also giving an account of what sport is as a social phenomenon. We have an understanding of there being boundaries between sport and related activities, such as games and dance, without committing to hard differences in the intrinsic natures of those activities.

4 Spectacle

Spectacle, the Spectacular and Spectating

Whether it be for good or ill, it is hard to deny that many of us have an appetite for spectacle. Our ancestors gathered to see gladiatorial battles, public executions, dramas acted on the stage, circuses, political rallies and ships launched to sea. The spectacular might not be to everyone's taste but has enough appeal to make circus performance a viable trade over a long history with a business model based on ticket sales. Spectator sports exploit this same human curiosity: a desire to see something remarkable; to witness exceptional human feats, to have all one's senses filled in an immersive and thrilling experience.

What is this spectacular experience? Let us take as exhibit A what is probably the most spectacular sporting event in the world: the World Cup Final of football. The 2018 men's competition saw France face Croatia in the final and they produced a classic game.

There is of course much ceremony around such a prestigious match. The golden trophy was unboxed for public view and the national anthems played before any sport began. Shorn of their training tops, we then had the visual delight of seeing a team in blue play against a team in red and white with a chequerboard on their front, set against the background of a luscious green pitch. There is an immediate aesthetic appeal with such vivid colours on show even if one understands little about the sport being played. The crowd in the stadium also contributes to the aesthetic, both as a visual backdrop but also for the noise that they produce, one which responds to the moments of excitement on the pitch. The spectacle of sport is not only visual even if it is primarily so. For those who attend games in person, they will also remember the smell of the grass and the thousands around them. There will be a sensory overload that many love, although it's not for everyone. The game is then underway and an unscripted drama is acted out.

Players dash around at top speed, clearly fitter than almost all of those watching. They are skilled too, quickly passing the ball to teammates and keeping possession against a similarly able opposition. There are some fast and neat passes but also arching long balls played accurately over distance. Crosses hang in the air, contested when opponents rise together, high off the ground, seeking to get a head on it. However, not all is so aesthetic and delicate. There are also some hard and tough contests, which at times are almost like wrestling. Football is a game of strength with hard tackles and opponents trying to stay the right side of the law as they push and jostle for space. We see an explicitly physical contest in all respects: a quest for dominance over the opponent.

The 2018 final also saw plenty of goals. Football is a low-scoring sport where three goals in a game is already above the average. With so few goals, each one is significant. Goals determine winners and thus each one becomes the moment of supreme spectacle. Some are more spectacular than others, and this final had some gems. Mario Mandžukić put into his own net for the opener, rising highest in an attempt to clear an Antoine Greizmann cross but inadvertently deflecting it past his own goalkeeper to give France the lead. This was soon matched when Ivan Perišić smashed a shot in from sixteen metres, across the keeper and inside the far post. A turning point in the game was the award of a soft penalty to France just before half time. This was a tense moment as the referee considered video evidence before deciding that a Croatian defender had cleared the ball with his hand. Griezmann tucked away the spot kick. Two fabulous strikes from distance proved decisive in the second half as first Paul Pogba and then Kylian Mbappé scored from distance, the ball thundering home and bulging the net on both occasions. Just a few minutes later, Mandžukić made a game of it again, though, by capitalising on a goalkeeper error to make it 4–2. There was no further score, however, and it was France who lifted the gleaming trophy during a lengthy closing ceremony. As well as the 78,000 watching in the stadium, there was a global TV audience of 1.12 billion.

There was spectacle. Roughly a seventh of the world's population shared an experience, looking at the same thing. There are few events outside of sport that could command so much of the world's simultaneous attention. If sport is in the business of creating a spectacle that people want to see, it is doing a good job. Is that what sport is really about, though? So far we have been considering physicality, competition and games. Sport seemed to be a combination of those elements. Would we want to add that it is also about creating spectacle? Or, rather, is it a mere by-product of sport that we want to watch it?

Looking and Enjoying

Setting aside that question, for the moment, it will be good to understand why it is such a pleasure to watch sport in which we are not participants. First, though, a clarification. I realise that I am posing this question with reference to just one sense faculty while I know that many unsighted people enjoy sport spectatorship too and that those with sight enjoy it with their other senses also. What I say can thus be understood to apply to other ways of perceiving sport, *mutatis mutandis*. Part of the spectacle is a sound spectacle, for instance. Most sports will have a typical sound.

An explanation could concern spectacle in general and apply just as much to non-sports. The theatre provides a spectacle, for instance, similarly with bright colours and lights and extraordinary events unfolding before us. This captivates us since the exceptional makes a greater impression on us than mundane, everyday experiences. There is also a social aspect in which groups of people gathering together for a shared experience is an addition to the spectacle, inside a theatre building, for example, increasing the intensity of the feeling.

What, however, would be distinctive about sport that would explain its particular appeal to the viewer and its notable success in attracting mass audiences? Is there something unique about sport's appeal or is it just another instance of what appeals to us in general? I will consider a couple of possible answers to this question that identify a special feature of sport as making it particularly apt for spectatorship. After that, however, I will develop a thesis that turns the account on its head.

The first answer to why there might be something special about sport, that makes it especially apt to produce pleasure when watched, follows from the idea developed in Chapter 1, that it is pleasurable to exercise our physical capabilities. Can we reasonably extend this thesis to a claim that it is pleasurable to witness others exercise their physical capabilities, without exercising one's own?

What might that be based upon? One idea could be that seeing others exercise their abilities brings us vicarious pleasure since it connects with the exercise of our own abilities. Perhaps this is even more important when one sees the exercise of an ability that one has lost or has never had to the degree witnessed. For instance, I know the joy of running at speed from when I was younger, when I could run hard, feeling the reserves of power in my legs and the air rushing by. Now it is not so easy but when I see others running with ease, it reminds me of the pleasures and feelings that I used to have. Sometimes the vicarious experience of sport can be instinctive and immediate. When I saw Mo Farah coming down the home straight at the 2012 Olympics to win gold, I could feel my own legs twitching as I tried to put in an additional kick for him. I was so absorbed in his trying to hold off any late challenge that I almost replicated some of his own movements. Perhaps I bent my chest forward to dip, just as he reached the finishing line. A vicarious experience is one you have through someone else's body, in some way putting yourself in their place, and feeling what they feel. There is a lot about this to understand, but if the possibility makes sense at all then it could explain how we take enjoyment from others exercising their capacities.

It can be easier to have vicarious experiences when one is able to identify with the person undergoing the original experience. I am pleased when a friend gets good news, for example, but less pleased the more distant my relationship is to the recipient of the news. How, then, is it that I can gain vicarious pleasure from someone performing sport, especially when it is someone I have never met or where they exercise an ability that I don't have? Identification could still be important, despite this, however. I am more likely to take vicarious pleasure from someone who I want to do well, for any reason; for example, someone who represents my own country or plays for the team that I support. Thus, I can really enjoy the feeling of clearing the bar in high jump, feeling some movements in my own body as I rehearse to clear the bar myself, when it is a competitor I want to do well. When a rival has their turn, I feel it less so. Now, of course, I don't know what it's like to run 100 metres in less than ten seconds but still I can take pleasure in seeing someone else doing so. Is this, then, because I can identify with them to at least some extent? And how weak can that extent be? Would it be enough for the identification to be by virtue of something as little as belonging to the same species? Are their achievements, in some distantly vicarious sense, then my achievements?

While such an experience might add to the pleasure of seeing someone exercise their abilities, perhaps it is not a necessary condition of taking pleasure in seeing what physical achievements another can achieve. Suppose I cannot even swim and find it virtually impossible to see myself in the place of a competitive swimmer. Maybe I've never even been to a pool and cannot imagine the smell of the chlorine or the feel of cutting through the water. Is it still not possible that I can admire their skill just for what it is? I can be impressed, for instance, when I see some skill that I never had and never want. I can be impressed even when I see a praying mantis eat a live scorpion, head first, although I neither identify with the praying mantis nor want its skill. I can also have a sense of discovery when I see a skill that didn't seem possible, for example, if I witness someone juggling balls while walking a tightrope. Seeing skilful feats can reward me with a sense of freedom as I experience what is possible. Even if I think it is not possible for me personally, as in the case of a successful pole vault, which I am sure I could not do, the depersonalised sense of freedom can still be impressed upon me.

There are then also the aesthetic pleasures to be taken from seeing someone else's skilful execution of an ability. The aesthetics of sport is a topic that deserves far greater discussion than I will give it here, but it is clear that there is an aesthetic appeal to sport. I won't go into detail on all the different types of aesthetic value to be found in sport (for that, my *Watching Sport*, 2011, is somewhere to start) but I will describe here how we can admire an athlete aesthetic-ally. We will have to stay silent on the origin of aesthetic value and content ourselves with the evident fact that there is such value. Then we can find that more aesthetic value is found in skilful execution of abilities than in clumsy and unskilful or unsuccessful execution of those abilities. A sprint runner has poise and grace. Her body exhibits power, speed and extension and these all appeal to our aesthetic sense. In contrast, the uncoordinated, asymmetric and inefficient style of a novice runner does not.

We have a number of reasons, therefore, for why it is pleasurable to watch another exercise their physical capacities. There are aesthetic reasons but we can also find it impressive, a discovery and liberation, as well as the vicarious experiences it gives us when we watch sport. These reasons focus on watching the actions and abilities of individual athletes, of the sort we considered in Chapter 1.

Permission to Enjoy

In Chapter 2, however, we looked at another important aspect of sport, which was competition. Might it be that we also take pleasure in seeing competition between others, even when we are not participants in that contest? Again, there could be a vicarious pleasure in doing so. Some of the same arguments mentioned above can be brought to the case of competition. One can sometimes feel a part of the victory if one identifies in some way with the winner. One can share some of Dina Asher-Smith's glory, for instance, if one is a compatriot. If you are from Sheffield, then the successes of Sheffield United also reflect on you. You can identify with the team because they are from your home city: you have allied to them and supported them, and so on.

This is, of course, tenuous. A team might consist of players entirely from outside the city they represent. Apart from cheering them on, the spectator might make virtually no contribution to the team's success. Nevertheless, it is clear that there is some basking in reflected glory (BIRGing) in the case of sports fans. That one is from the same nation as the winner, or merely in virtue of being a supporter, one is entitled to enjoy some of that glory. Sport can be a low-stakes hobby to the casual spectator since there is also the option of cutting off from reflected failure (CORFing). Victory and defeat are not symmetrical, then, since one can associate with the successes and dissociate from the failures.

It is not all just about victory and defeat, however, since clearly there is some attraction in the competition itself, prior to its result. By emotionally investing in one side or competitor, a viewer also experiences the excitement of the contest, knowing that some possible BIRGing awaits as the reward. Suppose one does not choose sides, however. Many people watch sport from a neutral perspective. Is there still pleasure to be taken in the competition? Arguably, yes. Then one can enjoy the drama of competition and, in particular, its facility to bring out peak performances from the rivals. In watching an Olympics or a football World Cup, one will see many contests in which it's not possible to find a personal interest, but one can appreciate that competitions of this stature will be those that athletes have planned their efforts around so that they can, all being well, produce their very best performances. Where we have closely matched opponents, we can sometimes get the best contests of all, perhaps where the eventual winner is uncertain until the very end. The viewer might not care which opponent wins but still enjoy the standard of performance the contest elicits and the twists and turns of the unfolding drama. For anxious viewers, watching with no interest in the winner might even be preferable since there will be no defeat from which one has to CORF.

There is one further aspect of the pleasure in watching competition that should not remain unstated. In Chapter 2 we noted that one function of sport was to provide a harmless space or bubble in which competition could occur where no one died from losing, unlike some other forms of competition, such as war. We can see that this applies also to the case of watching sport. It would be perverse to take pleasure in watching a competition where the losing opponent was to suffer real harm. It was wrong, for instance, to watch slaves being eaten by lions when they lost their 'contest' in the Roman Coliseum. Similarly, it would be wrong to watch with pleasure a tug-of-war tussle that one knew was contested over a deep ravine. No one's life is at stake in sport but competition still incentivises best performances. Fighting for one's life is an even bigger incentive and one might expect the very best performances of all to come from it. Even if that were so, however, it would still be wrong to enjoy those performances as spectators. Sport is a safe space in which there is permission to enjoy the spectacle for anyone watching. As in the case of theatre, a reason for this is that the performances are delivered voluntarily by all the performers, hence the autonomy of athletes (and actors) is respected by those watching (perhaps with some limitations, as we will see in the next chapter). One can enjoy seeing the competitions in sport and it is appropriate to bask in the glory of a win, which it would not be if the victory had been obtained at the cost of someone's harm, demise or ruin. The loser suffers some kind of defeat, of course, but it is one they have consented to take, in the event of the contest going a certain way, and it is one in which they should remain relatively safe.

The Evolution of Sport

Until this point we have been engaged in a project of describing the nature of sport. Competition, games and physicality have been the focus. However, there is a possible criticism of the approach thus far when it comes to the issue of spectatorship. This discussion has proceeded as if we can first provide an adequate theory of sport, as the institutionalised form of competitive physical games, and then move on to consider why it is pleasurable to watch such sports. Some answers to this latter question have already been provided above.

This is misconceived, however, if it means that the attractiveness to its audience is a merely contingent feature of sport, as if one could give an adequate theory of sport that made no reference to spectatorship. Many accounts of sport do exactly that. Now is the point of pivot, however: it is, instead, a necessary part of sport that it appeals to its spectators. Spectatorship, and the interests around it, are among the most important institutions that an institutional theory of sport must recognise. Spectatorship is thus a part of the ontology of sport: it is a significant part of what creates and validates a sport and directs its evolution. It is not that sport just happens to appeal to an audience, then. Rather, it was created to do so. Furthermore, the subsequent institutionalisation of sport has been, to a large extent, response dependent. By this I mean that those developments responded to what was appealing to its audience and thus able to sustain and grow its audience. It follows that if we really could take the spectators away from sport, then it would look quite different to how it looks now. A sport that was not meant to be watched would be an altogether alien invention and is not the sport that we have.

What is the justification for so bold a claim? In part this will be historical. The historical development of sport, I argue, supports the philosophical interpretation.

I have admitted that activities such as running, swimming and jumping have existed for as long as humanity has. When did sport arrive, though, as opposed to merely running and swimming, and as opposed to recreation and leisure? The answer is that it did so when there was the opportunity for enough people not just to play but also to consume sport in their free time, and to make it suitable for viewing. This occurred only after the industrial revolution had been established.

There were two types of sports-like activities prior to that time and which we should mention. First, there were the activities of the nobility: that tiny part of the population that had sufficient leisure time and wanted to exercise their physical capacities. We might put the game of real tennis in this category, a game played and watched by few, and which had no interest in attracting a wider audience. That would be the last thing the monarch would want. Such a game required wealth to own the space in which it could be played and to set up an adequate playing space.

More interesting is what was left for the commoners during this time, where the population earned a basic living, often at subsistence level, with little disposable income. Nevertheless, games were played, some of which have survived to the present day. Notable examples are the Shrovetide games of Ashbourne, Atherstone and Sedgefield and the game of Ba' in Orkney at New Year (see Hugh Hornby, *Uppies and Downies*, 2008). These were and continue to be mass participation games with few rules and long histories. They have largely resisted codification, though some rules have been introduced in more recent times, usually as a price to pay in return for the authorities allowing them to continue, despite the disruption and destruction they can cause. The Ashbourne game has emerged as the best known. It is played over two days each year, Shrove Tuesday and Ash Wednesday, from 14.00 to 22.00. It is contested between the Up'ards and Down'ards: all Ashbourne natives but divided between those born north and south of the River Henmore, which runs through the centre of the Derbyshire town. There are hundreds of players who turn out for each side. Their numbers are limited only by their willingness and there is no requirement that the sides be even. The large, custom-made and decorated ball is tossed up following an opening ceremony after which a brawl ensues as each side tries to gain possession. The game is rough, with plenty of bumps and bruises. It is not without danger, though there have been surprisingly few deaths among the players. The convention is that you can do anything you need to do in order to gain the ball but you should not injure an opponent deliberately. The purpose is to goal the ball but where the 'goals' are stone plinths emerging from the river over three miles apart at opposite ends of the town: the Up'ards' goal to the east and the Down'ards' goal to the south-west. To score, the ball must be tapped three times on a target in the centre of the plinth and this can only be done while standing knee deep in the cold water.

Participants find the game fun. They are passionate about it and its history. We can see, however, how completely unsuitable it is as a spectator sport. This is not to deny that tourists go to witness the occasion, but it is poor spectator sport nevertheless. In the first place, one is lucky to see the ball again after the toss-up since it often vanishes into the throng and one can only gain a close view by incurring personal risk. Even the film crews that occasionally visit struggle to get good footage. Then there is the duration. It is played without break over ten hours each day. There is no spectator sport like that. Even cricket has a shorter day's play and builds in lunch and tea breaks. Hardly anyone would bother trying to watch a whole day's play, even if they could always know where the ball was. There are moments of great excitement for the players, such as when the ball is handed to a runner who makes a dash for it. But one is more likely to witness a mass scrum in a ditch or the river or the ball trapped in some corner of a narrow street in the town, where it can remain stuck for hours. In this ten hours of play, goals are still rare. Only three can be scored in one day but sometimes 10 p.m. comes with no goals having been scored at all. One would think that with such a low-scoring game, and the difficulty with which play progresses, a goal will be extremely exciting to witness. It is indeed, for the participants, but even here there is little for any would-be spectator to see. Since the goal plinths are out in the country, and given the time it takes for the ball to get there, scoring most often occurs in total darkness with hardly any good vantage points where one could stay clean and dry. Few goals are adequately captured on film because of this. Things used to be even worse when the goals were inside mills (both of which have been demolished in the last six decades) since very few other people were able to squeeze inside and witness the scoring.

Ashbourne mass participation football has evolved a little, but such evolution was not in order to comply with the needs of spectatorship or media. The tradition is what counts to the town, some saying that the game is nine hundred years old. The earliest verified reference to the game is from 1683. There are several notable features in this short survey. There is little accommodation for the physical needs of spectators. There are no concessions at all to what would be interesting to watch. There are virtually no commercial interests with a stake in the game. Sponsorship is not especially sought. There are no formal structures for the players: no registration forms, no compensation process if injured, and so on. There is no outside jurisdiction: Ashbourne football is effectively a sporting law unto itself, independent of any connections to WADA, the IOC or even other festival football games around the country. And there is very little codification: just some basic conventions with tradition as the foremost custodian of the game. On that basis, it would be best not to classify

Ashbourne football as a sport. It is a physical game, and perhaps we might go as far as to think of it as a pre-sport, but there is much that would have to change for it to be recognised properly as a sport, which isn't going to happen.

By way of contrast, let us now consider what happened when football evolved into its current codified form and the differences this modern sport has to its mass participation predecessors. The first football club in the world formed in 1857 in Sheffield, in the middle of the Victorian era. The Sheffield Football Club had leisured gentlemen as members. Soon, other clubs began to form elsewhere, often adopting different rules. It took a while for standardisation to occur but gradually it did as agreements were reached on numbers of players per team, dimensions of the playing area, the markings on the pitch, size of the ball, duration of play, and so on. A single code was adopted. Concurrently, these smaller playing areas began to be enclosed so that admission could be charged for entry. Then, in the late nineteenth century and into the early twentieth, advances were made in stadium construction. Banks of terracing were laid and more people could gain a good view and were thus willing to pay the admission price. Archibald Leitch constructed grandstands that offered a better view with comfort and a roof. Such developments would be useless for the Ashbourne game.

Here is where the pivot point strikes. It is not a mere coincidence that the codification of the sport produced something that just so happened to be conducive to spectatorship. Instead, its developments were designed so that the sport could be attractive to an audience and thus commercially lucrative for its owners. This includes the limitation on the duration of a game, the pitch that offers an ideal balance between space for the play to expand and always being viewable from the side lines, and the stricter codification that allowed for a sense that the game was fair rather than arbitrary.

Like other sports battling for attention and the money it can bring, football has continued to change in ways it expects will make it more attractive. The teams wear colourful strips, goal nets are designed to make scoring look more spectacular, stadiums are planned by architects to be easy and comfortable to use but also to look good on TV. Rule changes are not common but usually intended to make the game more appealing to the viewer, whether that be on aesthetic grounds, such as the change to the back pass rule to the goalkeeper in the 1990s, or on grounds of fairness, with the introduction of video assistant refereeing (VAR).

Situated Sport

We have to accept that sport is a socially situated phenomenon. It may have begun as a form of individual and team exercise, or just for the joy of physicality, there for the good of its players, but now exists primarily for the interest of the complex web of commercial interests within which it sits. Fundamental to those commercial interests are the attentions of viewers. Getting paying customers into the stadium was initially the aim but the advent of pay TV, together with disposable income and leisure time, has directed those financial interests to a new kind of delivery, where there are now millions around the world with an interest and who are willing to consume sport at a distance.

In the battle for attention, football clearly is the winner, as the most popular spectator sport and therefore with the biggest commercial interests. Other sports have followed the same route, though, even if on a smaller scale. Hence, spectatorship is not apart from sport; it is integral to it. It determines the look of the sport, its schedule, its structure, the size of its prizes, the developments in its rules and also its financial inequalities. Individual athletes and sporting clubs, if they are popular, can attract bespoke television deals if they operate under a jurisdiction that permits it. This varies by sport and by national authority. Clearly there are dangers if the inequalities grow too large, however. If success in a team sport produces more success, then competitiveness becomes compromised. Over time, some sporting clubs can grow to be much bigger and richer than their rivals and come to dominate too much. Sports can be dull if the winners are the same year after year. This has become a structural problem for some sporting institutions since a balance has to be found between rewarding the victors and keeping interest alive in the sport. American football has rules that aim to level the contest by giving the worst sides from the previous year the first pick of new players that are available. This sort of rule remains rare but might be best for the long-term health of a sport.

Sport is not just embedded within its own sporting institutions. We have to be mindful that those institutions themselves exist within wider societal structures. Sport is a social phenomenon that reflects its own society. The fact that women's sports have been under-supported is likely to be a reflection of the wider values of the society in which sport is situated, for instance, which I will come back to in detail in Chapter 6.

In the Western world, sport was driven to attract spectators for commercial reasons. It is a commercial enterprise for all concerned and might be thought of as part of the entertainment industry but for the fact that its organisational structures and those of the entertainment industry (film, television, theatre, comic books and so on) have remained distinct. Sport could be situated within different social systems, however. In Soviet Russia sport was not encouraged for commercial reasons: at least not officially, since the USSR was supposedly a non-capitalist country. Still, interest in sport was desired by the authorities and one can see that there would be reasons to do so within that social system, such as propaganda, instilling national pride, diverting ordinary people from their personal situation, and so on. To an extent, these factors can play into the thinking in most countries anyway, even in those where the commercial interest is dominant. Every struggling political leader welcomes national sporting victories that improve the mood of the people and decrease discontent. For this reason, sporting organisations often receive government funding: not all of it comes from privately owned media companies. We must acknowledge, then, that the institutions of sport do not exist in isolation from the surrounding national and global institutions. The boundaries between social institutions are permeable.

We thus reach a very broad conception of the ontology of sport. What constitutes sport is not simply the individual competitive acts that opponents exercise in their attempt to win. Competitors are partaking in an activity that has been developed and evolved to satisfy other interests too. Those activities might have their basis in the pleasure of individuals in exercising their physical capacities. If no one was also interested in seeing them do so, however, then the practices around those physical capacities would look very different. Many people like to jog, swim or workout in the gym but they are not doing sport. They might be preparing for sport but they are not participating in the codified form of games that I have described. Even when one plays sport privately, such as when friends have a game of tennis with no audience, we have to acknowledge that the activity within which they are engaged is one whose entire form has been determined by the institutions of that sport with commercial interests in mind, which usually means for the purpose of attracting an audience. Private games occur, of course, whether for fun or for practice, but there remains a sense, even in cases like these, in which spectators are still there.

The key claim of this chapter is thus justified. It is no coincidence that sport is spectacular. It is designed exactly to be so. The sports that have succeeded on a commercial level will be those that have attracted the most attention. There is still a job for philosophy to do, however, in saying what specifically it is in the sport that attracts us, and I have attempted to do some of that. Sports tap into a broadly aesthetic appeal both in the individual athletic contests and in all that surrounds them. Those surroundings can be vital.

A large stadium with a packed crowd undoubtedly adds to the spectacle. At the opposite end of the scale, a sport like squash has clearly struggled to attract a mass spectatorship, primarily because it is played in an enclosed space. Those who play the sport might be content with its relatively low profile since it is a good competitive game in itself. Already there have been developments such as playing within a transparent court at championship level so that a larger audience can see, and TV cameras can get better angles. It remains to be seen whether this will allow squash to catch up with other sports in the size of its audience or whether it had too slow a start.

Perhaps I have not yet acknowledged all the complexities in the issue of spectatorship, especially when it occurs within a commercial context. Where financial interests exist, is there not the possibility of exploitative relations developing? Once sports are competing with each other for their share of the global audience, might there be temptations to do so in the wrong way? Consider how women's beach volleyball has so much of the athletes' exposed bodies on show, unnecessarily from a purely sporting perspective. This indicates that once sport is situated within our social practices it also becomes an ethically contested space. It is right, then, that we move on next to consider the ethics of sport.

5 Ethics

A Normative Space

Sport is full from top to bottom with normative notions and judgements: the team *deserved* to win; a player *should have* given the ball back; the referee's decision was *unfair*; a particular move was *against the spirit* of the game; an incident was *deceptive*, perhaps even *cheating*; someone did the *wrong* thing, or *right* thing; there was a *good* outcome. These are example of normative judgements where normativity concerns what *should* or *should not* be rather than what is. The normative, I maintain, does not merely intrude into sport. Rather, sport is an inherently ethical space, which concerns right and wrong, good and bad, and what ought to be.

Any complex, socially situated interaction between self and other is bound to be like this. When we think of sport in terms of desert, obligations, duties, fairness, freedoms, rights, cheats, deceits, dubious practices, playing it the right or wrong way, then we are putting sport under ethical scrutiny, viewing it through a normative lens. More than that, it can be argued that a shared set of norms are constitutive of 'good' sport to the extent that they are a precondition of fairness and the idea of play. In that case a sporting encounter is also an ethical encounter. When one enters a sporting engagement with another, one is not just under an athletic scrutiny but also an ethical scrutiny. You will be judged on how you perform physically and whether you win or not but also on whether you did the right thing throughout the contest. Losers can preserve their honour and winners can be disgraced. In extreme cases, egregiously inappropriate behaviour can end careers. Each sporting contest puts the athlete at such risk.

Why are sport and ethics tied so closely together? The groundwork has already been laid that can suggest a theory. We have noted, in previous chapters, that sport is a safe space in which competition can occur. Its prelusory goals are unimportant: being the other side of a bar; a golf ball being in a hole; a dart being in a board, and so on. This allows competition to be indulged where nothing vital is at stake since no one is really harmed even if they lose. You can then roundly defeat your opponent without doing them a wrong. The safety of the sporting encounter, understood in the way just described, creates for it an ethical bubble. Within this bubble there are some things you may do that you would not be permitted to do outside of the bubble. It looks, then, as if the bubble creates some degree of ethical licence. However, athletes enter into that bubble with a shared understanding of what is and is not permissible within it. Violating those agreed norms – even if the agreement is only implicit – is where approbation awaits. The risk is especially high given some of the actions that are permitted within the bubble and the liminal spaces athletes must traverse. Explaining and justifying this interpretation of sport is my business in the present chapter.

The Sporting Bubble

The difference between inside and outside the sporting bubble is illustrated with an example that is both unpleasant and disturbing. In 2001 a boxing match in New York between James Butler and Richard Grant concluded with a unanimous decision in favour of Grant. The fight was part of a 9/11 charity event and it had gone the distance with many blows traded. Grant celebrated the win and then went to commiserate Butler. As Grant offered an embrace, Butler, with his degloved hand, sucker-punched Grant, knocking him unconscious, loosening his jaw, dislodging teeth. Grant fell to the canvas, blood gushing from his wounded tongue. Just two minutes earlier, Butler and Grant had been punching each other for all they were worth, although wearing gloves and gumshields. The bout had concluded, however. The competitive encounter was now over. Butler and Grant had left the sporting bubble in which acts of punching were permitted. For committing an act that was no longer permissible, since they had moments earlier left the sporting bubble, Butler was led away by police, charged, and then served four months in prison.

The example starkly illustrates the difference that the bubble permits not least because it concerns boxing. All sporting encounters are competitions for dominance but this is particularly conspicuous in the case of boxing where opponents try to beat each other into submission. Things can happen in the ring that outside of it would get you arrested. As Butler found, it is not even simply a matter of being in or out of the ring that marks the boundary of the bubble. In entering the ring, one enters a liminal space. The sporting contest has an additional ritualised beginning, end and breaks, where the true boundary is marked. The clanging of the bell signals that the competitive encounter stops. No matter how involved the fight has become, with the bell one can no longer attempt to assert dominance.

How are we to understand this bubble, then, and in particular its ethical standing? In general terms, it is conducive to what philosopher of sport Bob Simon called internalism. This idea of internalism is that within the sporting contest there is a distinct set of values at work. There is an ethic that is internal to the sport and does not apply outside of it. This is striking in the case of boxing. One is permitted to punch someone during the sporting encounter but not once the competition stops. Examples from other sports will be less dramatic but the point still holds. If an opponent in a race slips and falls, one does not have to wait for them to get back up. One is permitted to take advantage of their misfortune, run on and win. Ordinary values outside of sport would suggest instead that you check on someone who falls, helping them back up and providing any required assistance. Simon does not believe that all the values within sport are unpleasant ones, however. There are others that are not strictly part of the rules but are nevertheless accepted as the correct way to play, such as returning a ball from a throw-in when the opposition have kicked it out for an injured player to receive treatment.

Overall, however, a less pleasant ethic seems to operate within the sporting bubble. Because competition is understood as a contest for dominance, it is possible to interpret sport as a fascistic encounter. The weak opponent who slips in competition is to be shown no mercy. Indeed, it violates an important norm of sport not to try one's absolute best to win. Competition is meant to distinguish the weak from the strong, one could say, and it is strength that is rewarded and celebrated. Defeat is designed to elicit shame in the weak. If sport indeed embodies fascistic values such as these, we might then say that it can be justified on the grounds given above: that it is a permissible way of doing so since nothing is really at stake. However, this would still be an unpleasant finding since we might wonder what it says about us that we have felt a need to create a quarantined space in which we can indulge fascistic tendencies. Why should we want to dominate other people at all, even safely? And would sports enthusiasts be tarnished by their interest in an essentially fascistic encounter?

Sport might well rest on a grim premise. Before we face the difficult questions that would arise if so, however, we should also consider whether there are more sympathetic interpretations of the sporting bubble.

First of all, the internalist interpretation of its ethics can be challenged. The alternative would be to say that the ethics of sport are continuous with, rather than separate from, the ethics of the wider society within which sport is situated. A continuity thesis need not mean that the ethics of sport are exactly the same as those outside sport but only that there can be an overlap and influences in either direction: general ethical frameworks can influence ethics in sport and vice versa. Let us look at how that might work.

In the first place, if we accept that the practice of sport is embedded within wider social institutions, then we should expect sport to be ethically porous with respect to the values of those institutions. The institutional theory of sport fits with this, of course. To take the example of one such social institution, the advertising industry, then we will expect an influence from that industry to be present in sport. Sponsorships will be attractive to advertisers only if the sport is able to reflect the values with which the sponsoring company wishes to be associated. In order to sell products, commercial interests are unlikely to want to be associated with a fascistic practice, since potential customers might not like that. However, this is itself dependent on the broader institutions that drive the values of society. There are occasions when nations are themselves overtaken by fascistic values, which might then gain free rein in sport. We are not quite in that situation yet (as I write in 2020) so I would not expect many institutional interests to influence sport in a fascistic direction. Instead, I would expect influences that encourage good, positive and supporting values in sport: that it be organised in a fair and enhancing way, for instance. Gladiatorial mortal combat might have been endorsed by the Roman Empire but we now expect better.

Second, can we expect that some of the values of sport then return to enhance the society in which it is situated? According to some views, we can. One idea is that the sporting bubble can be used as a moral laboratory. Again, exploiting the essential harmlessness of sport's prelusory goals, we can see sport as running a series of experiments in which our values are tested. In particular, we can pitch various virtues and vices against each other and see which succeed. The outcomes could then inform norms that are useful outside of sporting contexts. In team sports, for example, we see how teams that can collaborate well, and behave as cohesive units, tend to be successful relative to those in which individualism dominates. That is an ethical lesson that is applicable beyond sporting contexts, wherever collaboration is undertaken. Mike McNamee (*Sports, Virtues and Vices*, 2008) makes a similar point, presenting sporting encounters as a new form of morality play, imparting moral lessons to its viewers.

If there is something in a continuity thesis then we might have a reply to those who emphasise dominance as an aim in sport, and draw conclusions to its fascist nature. Dominance might sound fascistic in the abstract but now we can consider sport in its social context, interacting with the prevalent values of its context. Sport is not, after all, a gladiatorial contest to the death. It occurs within an agreed framework, with safeguards, where participation should be voluntary and where fun can occur. As noted previously, some enjoy competition and feel that it allows them to produce their best performances by incentivising the maximum exercise of their capacities. Within that framework, sport can be justified as a positive social practice on the ground that it contributes to human flourishing (Sigmund Loland, *Fair Play in Sport*, 2002).

We should acknowledge, however, that ethical issues arise not simply within the sporting bubble but in virtue of the existence of the bubble itself. The protected safe space in which competition occurs over inconsequential goals has facilitated the rise of a number of ethically problematic developments. Among these, we can include the betting industry. Gambling is supported by, and in turn supports through sponsorships, an activity that is capable of producing addictions. We have fan violence, nationalism, parochialism, racism, sexism, homophobia and various forms of corruption: match fixing, betting conspiracies, political interference, performance enhancement and potential bribery for rights to host lucrative events. The existence of sport might contribute to human flourishing, as Sigmund Loland says. It might give many people pleasure. Balanced against that, however, we have to acknowledge that sport is at the centre of many ethically dubious practices.

An excuse could be that this is determined primarily by sport's financial significance, since crime and corruption often follows money. If we acknowledge the continuity thesis, then of course social and personal vices will appear within and around sport. Nevertheless, it has also to be acknowledged that certain arrangements within the structure of sport facilitate these practices too. Sport provides clear but not entirely predictable results, which are exactly the things people can be induced to bet upon. Sport has an oppositional structure that lends itself to conflict among spectators. We cannot blame fan violence solely on sport since it no doubt reflects the violent tendencies inherent in society. But it is more than pure chance that violent cultures have become attached to sport spectatorship, where there are winners and losers, more than they have to, for example, the theatre.

Fairness

I will now turn to three issues that will allow us to understand the ethical significance and impact of the sporting bubble better. These are issues around fairness, harm to the athlete and the athlete voice.

Fairness first. Fairness is clearly of importance to those playing and watching sport. Defeats can be accepted but only if they are thought of as fair. Similarly, a win that is judged to be unfair is tarnished. Fairness is not simply a legal notion. If a victory is aided by rule-breaking, that clearly is unfair but there are cases of unfairness where rules are not broken. Suppose a runner is allocated a lane to run in that is disadvantageous compared to the others. There is a pool of water standing in it, for instance. This is not the fault of any of the rival athletes, who have no control over it and are not breaking any rules. It would be reasonable to object to the lane, nevertheless, on the grounds of fairness.

The metaphor of a level playing field is an instance where an ethical precept of sport has spread to wider society and appears frequently in non-sporting contexts. If one team had to play a whole game uphill, hence the other team played it all downhill, that would not be fair, which seems to be the literal case upon which the metaphor is based. We can apply the principle outside sport, for instance when we say that everyone should be treated the same under the law, irrespective of race, gender or sexuality.

It is clear, however, that the metaphor does not convey enough of what fairness means in sport. If by the level playing field we mean that all competitors have an equal opportunity to win, then that clearly is false. We do not have, and nor do we want, that in sport. If we wanted to achieve that, we would give slower runners a head start or weaker gymnasts a wider beam to walk on. That is not the point of sport, however. It is not about giving everyone the same chance of winning each contest, nor do we want all the athletes to finish at the same time, achieve the same distance, record the same score, and so on. Rather, sport should provide an opportunity for the participants to display their inequality: that one can run faster than the others, throw a javelin further, gain more heptathlon points, perform the best floor routine, score more goals, and so on.

Should we say, then, that the level playing field is about everyone having the same opportunity to manifest their personal potential, allowing that different people have different potentials? A runner might be able to complete the 200 metres in twenty seconds but not if thirty metres of their lane is under an inch of water. Instead, we should aim to provide optimum conditions for the athletes, consistent with the unnecessary obstacles dictated by the rules. If we cannot quite achieve optimum conditions, since they are not all within our control, we should at least seek the same conditions for the participants. It is wrong for one to have either more advantages or disadvantages than the others.

This is a better account, but still not quite what we mean by a level playing field. For a start, it ignores the place of chance in sport. Good luck and bad luck occur and we tolerate it. If one 200-metre runner starts well, but halfway round the bend a bird flies directly towards her, causing her to flinch and slow down slightly, then she has not had the same opportunity as the others to display her ability. This is out of our control, however. It's unlucky but it's not unfair. We might try to legislate for outside interferences, as football has done, but we cannot stop them all. Play isn't suspended if a goalkeeper has the sun in her eyes, for instance, though she might feel that it's unlucky if it causes her to concede a goal. Similarly in rugby, the shape of the ball introduces an element of chance and one side might get an unlucky bounce that stops them from doing what they had the potential to do if the bounce had been better.

A second reason why the level playing field is not simply about equality of opportunity is that this notion is itself problematic. When we use terms such as 'opportunity' and 'potential', there is a vital ambiguity to note. A sporting contest might give its competitors the opportunity to manifest *their* own ability. Not everyone has the same level of ability, however, and in that sense they do not all have the same opportunity to win. While this might seem like a pedantic point, it is crucial in our understanding of the level playing field. There is not a level playing field in sport to the extent that the competitors will have received the same opportunities to develop their ability prior to the contest. It is clear that there are many social determinants of athletic health, strength and fitness, and we know that some will have received better training, nutrition and equipment than others because they come from wealthier backgrounds. The consistent domination of the Olympic medals tables by the USA might ultimately indicate their advantage of wealth and privilege over other nations more than simply a sporting one. The point suggests that sporting success and historical economic success are therefore hard to disentangle. There is this obvious sense, then, in which the level playing field is not about ensuring equality of opportunity.

What is left, if anything, of our notion of fairness? Should we judge it to be only a myth, perhaps one that attempts to hide the fact that inequalities determine sporting outcomes? We might then have doubts about it as an ethical principle. After all, who dictates what counts as fair within a sporting contest when nudging an opponent away from the ball is deemed to be unfair but having a vastly rich owner who can afford to buy all the best players and give them the highest salaries and best facilities is entirely fair? Who controls that narrative or fairness?

Lest we give up on the notion of fairness in sport, however, a more constructive account is possible. This can provide a serviceable concept of fairness: one that we can apply usefully in sporting contexts. After all, we do seem to have some use for a notion of fairness even though we know that there are many inequalities in sport. It will help if we abandon the metaphor of the level playing field and instead think of the issue in terms of consent.

This account of fairness will be applicable specifically to fair play rather than fairness more generally. These two can come apart and what I say applies only to the former. It is possible that two sides play a game of hockey entirely fairly but where the outcome is widely considered to be unfair. The kind of situation I identify here is where the side that had most of the play and created the best chances nevertheless loses. This is possible in sport and is accepted because at least some degree of uncertainty of outcome is desirable. That kind of fairness concerns desert. Fair play is different and concerns the tacit understanding of the participants in sport. Sports are competitive contests, as we have noted. We have also seen that within the sporting bubble, acts are sometimes permitted that would not be permitted outside of it. In the extreme example of boxing, opponents punch each other. Nevertheless, even in this violent sport there is a sense of fair play. Punches to the face and stomach are fair. Punches below the belt are not, or punches thrown after the bell has sounded at the end of the round. How are we allowed to treat another person this way and how are fair and unfair distinguished in sport?

The solution lies in the consent, freedom and autonomy of the participants. This account seems applicable to all sports and not just those where one could suffer harm. It is essential that all competitors enter the contest freely, and maintain their autonomy throughout, such that they could stop playing if they wish. It must be a *voluntary* attempt to overcome the unnecessary obstacles since participation carries a risk of defeat. Consent can only be given, however, if one knows to what one is consenting. If I agree to a contest on the expectation that it will be by breaststroke but arrive to find that it is butterfly, then I have no obligation to continue. This applies to smaller but still significant violations of the shared understanding of that sport. Sprint runners enter the contest on an assumption that all eight lanes are physically equivalent. Elite football is played now on an assumption that goal-line technology is in use and reliable. Charges of unfairness can be grounded on any deviations from these assumptions.

Those examples concerned the conditions under which the sport is played, but assumptions also relate to the conduct that is expected of opponents. Pugilists agree to a contest in boxing. In agreeing to fight Mike Tyson, Evander Holyfield did not consent to have his ear bitten off since ear biting is not a part of the sport in which the opponents agreed to partake. We can see that this follows from Suits's account of lusory goals. The aim is to stop the opponent by punching them, not by biting them. Similarly, in entering a 200-metre race, one is agreeing to stay on the track. One cannot run across the infield to cut the corner, nor can one reach out and pull an opponent back by their vest. Participation is assumed to be on the basis of agreed conduct.

Because the shared understanding of the norms of a sport is often only tacit, there will be cases where a competitor pushes at the limits of those norms. There are controversies around 'sledging' in cricket, for instance, where an opponent delivers a persistent barrage of insults to distract and undermine the confidence of a player. Some degree of it seems accepted now as part of the game, hence one has consented to its possibility in agreeing to play. It must have limits, however. No one consented to be racially abused in playing sport and nor should they ever be obliged to do so. A compelled consent, after all, would not really be consent at all. There are occasional instances of players leaving games when they receive racist abuse, whether this be from opponents or spectators. It is not unknown for them to be sanctioned for doing so. The account I have given is one in which we have to respect the autonomy of the athlete as a precondition of competition. They agree not just to compete *simpliciter*, but to compete in a certain way, obeying the rules, norms and conventions of the sport. Consent to compete is not given as a one-off action that then applies for all time, however. It is effectively given before every competitive encounter, at the point at which the athlete freely enters the sporting bubble. That consent is actively reaffirmed in every sporting action; in continuing to play the game. It follows that consent can be withdrawn at any moment if what occurs violates the agreement. This does not mean that a team can walk off just because they are losing. They consented to the possibility of defeat. But there are many things to which they clearly have not consented. Tyson was deducted a point for biting off part of Holyfield's ear. That was a woefully inadequate punishment and Holyfield was within his rights to have left the contest, as would be anyone who experienced racism or misogyny while playing.

Athlete Harm

Now let us move from athletes as ethical agents to athletes as ethical subjects, in particular as the recipients of unethical acts. Racism is one harm that can be experienced in sport. Physical injury such as losing an ear is another. What other harms does an athlete risk? I will again consider this question in relation to consent since I think, first, consent casts a helpful light on the problem of athlete harm and, second, the place of harm in sport shows that consent is not a simple matter.

It is clear that our athletes are harmed directly in a range of sports. In boxing, rugby, football and combat sports there is a high possibility of pain being inflicted immediately but also long-term injuries being incurred. Head injuries and broken legs are serious and some are career-ending. Some sports accept concussions as par for the course. The responses of the relevant sporting organisations seem to focus on mitigation with safeguards against the possibility of injury and then protocols in place for when they occur. It could at least be argued that these mitigations are part of the shared understanding of the sporting encounter when an athlete consents to participate; that is, the athlete agrees to participate in a contest aware of the risks and the mitigations that are in place. Matters are more complicated than that, however.

The point will be better taken if we look at other forms of harm that athletes might suffer. Typically, the system of mitigation is only in place for in-career injuries. The support protocols apply only when one is within the sporting bubble or at least the associated industry. Athletes can do long-term harm to their bodies, however, and create health problems that persist long after they have left their clubs or coaches. Consider tennis star Andy Murray, who has gone public about the pain that is now a part of his daily life. Murray struggled with back and hip injuries towards the end of his career. It now seems likely that he continued in tennis beyond a point where it was wise to do so from a purely health point of view. Clearly there were motivations to do so – perhaps even pressures – but we have to wonder whether the athlete himself fully understood the risks. Consider also the evidence, though this is still far from conclusive, that some professional footballers have received brain damage from persistently heading the ball, leading to serious health problems after retirement. Is this something to which they consented in virtue of playing this game? Suppose participation in a sport were shown to contribute to serious deteriorative diseases. Should it even be possible to consent to this? Athletes do sometimes consent to high risks that they seemingly understand. But should we let a young person harm their future self even if they are fully informed?

There are some other forms of harm to be acknowledged too, which might be overlooked since they do not involve physical harm. The harm can be just as damaging, however. The rewards of becoming an elite athlete are so huge that many are attracted to it as a career. Inevitably, these will almost all be young people since most top-level sports require an early entry if one is to have a chance of becoming professional. The sport is then in the advantageous position of more wanting to be elite players than are needed, with the inevitable consequence that the vast majority of candidates can be discarded as the very best are chosen. This is a harm that sport does to its athletes; not just in dashing their hopes but also with the effect of damaging their future prospects as other career avenues are neglected in pursuit of the dream. Is there adequate care and support for young adults who must suddenly adapt to a different kind of life from the one for which they had been preparing?

There are even more intangible harms in sport. Consider the commodification and objectification of athletes. Players are bought and sold, not just by sporting clubs but by sponsoring brands. They belong to an industry that requires a return on its investment, from a programme to which they signed up while still young. Now part of the system and objectified, they have to accept the athletic examination: be available as near perfect physical specimens to our sporting gaze but not to trouble us with their personal opinions. Objectification is a way of denying someone's humanity and sport does seem to have a propensity for focusing on the physical attributes of the athlete. This attitude denies the athlete their agency; an autonomy that we feel every human should have. Are athletes not human, then? More urgently, if we deny athletes their autonomy, how can we also claim that consent is the principle that determines their sporting participation?

These forms of athlete harm have the effect of problematising consent. Superficially, consent looks to be a simple act of agreement. We know, however, that there have to be conditions attached if it is to be valid. It has to be *informed* consent. The cases above show, however, that not all the relevant information is available to the athlete, or that they are not in an ideal position to understand it, not least because they embarked on a career while young. There is an age of sexual consent for very good reasons. One can be considered too immature to give consent. There is not, however, a corresponding age of sporting consent even though some of the same considerations carry over. If consent is compromised, then, so too would be the notion of fair play in sport, which rests upon consent. These are difficult issues, admittedly. Nevertheless, it is tempting to think that the sporting industry itself is happy to pay no more than superficial attention to them. Commercially, sport is a highly successful industry with no shortage of human capital. There is little incentive to worry about the many who sport discards. It is all the more important, then, that we have those difficult conversations in other spaces and start to take the interests of athletes seriously. In particular, if consent is a precondition of any sporting contest at all, then we have to nurture and defend the athlete's autonomy. We have to listen to their experiences and take them seriously.

The Athlete Voice

This brings us to the athlete voice. There is a danger of this subject being considered only a peripheral issue compared to all the complicated ethical challenges that sport faces: pressing issues for the integrity of the sport, such as the use of performance enhancements. Nevertheless, the athlete voice is central to the ethical debates within sport. We have built an argument in which sport is a safe space for competition wherein acts are permitted that would not be permitted outside. The legitimacy of the sporting bubble requires that entry is on a consensual basis. One consents to compete under a set of conditions, and the consent of all generates a shared understanding of what the sporting encounter involves. This led us to understand consent as the basis of fairness in sport but where we see that consent is legitimate only if it acknowledges the autonomy of the athlete to give it freely.

We only have consent, then, if we acknowledge an athlete's interests so that they can withdraw consent if they wish, can question the terms under which they are granting the consent, and have their free agency recognised. This is to acknowledge the most obvious datum of sport: that it is played by human beings. The athlete voice is a more contentious matter than it needs to be because there are some powerful interests that question whether the athlete should have a voice at all. The autonomy of athletes is denied when they face sanctions for speaking up. Colin Kaepernick was frozen out of his sport for taking a knee during the national anthem in protest against racism. President Trump had previously declared that football players should be fired for taking part in such a protest. Are athletes expected to have no political opinions, to tolerate injustices from which they suffer, or to express no political opinions when everyone else is permitted to do so? Why? Evidently, there is such fear of athletes speaking out that the IOC are attempting to ban all political statements from Olympic competitors under their proposed new rule 50.

Now it might be said that politics and sport should not mix and just because someone excels at sport they have no right to pronounce on political issues. Apart from denying athletes their freedom of speech, however, and threatening their autonomy on that basis, one should also question why this vocation in particular is singled out as having to be apolitical. It is not as if they are civil servants whose professional role requires political neutrality. Besides, is there a sharp divide between the political and the non-political? Who decides what is political and what is not? Why is it political to endorse racial or gender equality but not to endorse McDonald's and Coca-Cola, which sporting events do when those companies provide sponsorship? Deciding what is or isn't political is itself a political act: usually one reserved for the politically powerful. Might the real issue, then, be that the institutions of sport fear the potential power of the athlete voice?

Top athletes have a high profile. Their statements, even about non-sporting matters, can carry a lot of weight. As an example, consider Marcus Rashford's successful campaign in 2020 to extend free school dinners for underprivileged children to the summer holidays. The British government ignored such calls for weeks until Rashford's intervention. With his 2.9 million Twitter followers and access to mainstream media, his voice was heard far and wide, exerting a pressure on the government that even the official opposition in Parliament could not attain. It is understandable why other forms of power could fear this kind of influence and seek to undermine its legitimacy.

This includes the powers within the sporting institutions themselves. It is especially taboo to threaten the interests of the status quo and the organisations that have financial interests in sport: for instance, if an athlete were to criticise a major financial contributor to sport for their ethical record. Sports sometimes organise their own official causes, such as the Let's Kick Racism Out of Football campaign in the UK. This again undermines the autonomy of the individual athlete, however, who is expected to promote these official causes but is not given autonomy to raise their own. The greatest wrath is reserved for anyone who speaks against the institutions of sport themselves, such as Megan Rapinoe, who has consistently fought the gender pay gap (and was the first white athlete to take a knee after Kaepernick, in solidarity). Along with her team mates, she has even filed a law suit against the United States Soccer Federation on the grounds of gender discrimination, putting her political voice in direct legal conflict with the organisation under whose jurisdiction she falls in her professional life.

We have to acknowledge that athletes are at the wrong end of an essentially exploitative relationship. Many are exploited with no reward at all, offering their efforts gratis in the hope of making it to the big time. In the majority of instances, these athletes are cast aside. Even those who receive rich rewards are still exploited. Salaries can look immense but, even here, the profits to be made in elite sports far outweigh the portion that is given back to the athletes. The owners and institutions take their share. Certainly sport is organised so that its athletes receive expensive support, but we should not think of this being purely to assist their flourishing. An investment is made and there is an expected return on investment. Alongside a financial exploitation, there are other forms of exploitation that spring from power imbalances. Athletes know that to succeed, they have to cooperate with the system and do as they are told in all things from diet, bedtime and, of course, exercise regime. Enough cases have been documented to show that physical and even sexual abuse can occur when athletes are subjected to those powerful influences in their lives. A culture in which their voices are silenced facilitates this.

Giving athletes a greater voice will not solve all of these problems. Part of my argument is that athletes are in a vulnerable position, often not knowing what is best for themselves or their future selves and having to rely on the very industry that exploits them as their source of information. It can put further pressure on an athlete if they are treated as role models when they are not comfortable with that position. Megan Rapinoe and Marcus Rashford are willing to speak up on controversial issues, but we cannot make it an expectation. For the good of the athlete, however, we must create a safe enough space for them to speak out. It is they, after all, who have the most immediate experiences of unethical practices within and around sport.

Accounts of ethics in sport often focus on personal failings of individual athletes, if we look at issues of cheating and drug-taking, for instance. In this chapter, however, I have tried to take a broader perspective on the ethical credentials of sport itself. What comes into view is that athletes are not so much agents of the unethical as they are on the receiving end of it. Even in those cases where athletes are caught doing wrong, we have to consider what within the organisation of sport facilitated, or even encouraged, such actions.

6   Inclusion

Sport for All?

The question of inclusion is among the most urgent of ethical concerns currently in sport and warrants a chapter of its own. There have been campaigns to encourage greater participation in sport, especially among groups that were already under-represented. A Sport for All campaign ran in the seventies and eightiess promoting the idea of sport as potentially a positive influence on anyone's life, regardless of their level of ability. I shall examine the argument for this claim. I will then go on to consider some of the key groups who historically have been excluded, namely, disabled people and women. In the case of the latter, I will then consider some of the biggest current controversies in sport: the place of women with differences of sex development and sport for trans athletes. Questions of eligibility are raised here and we need to understand what is behind those questions. Concerns regarding trans athletes seem part of a general moral panic around the status of trans people and, while I accept that this is a contentious issue, I will not shy away from coming down firmly on one side of the debate. I try to do so in a reasoned way.

Apart from current trends in the debate, there is another reason why I have to address questions of inclusion. In Chapter 1 I started my account of sport by emphasising the importance of abilities, with sport being an arena in which one can develop and exercise one's physical capacities. Might this account, then, be an inherently ableist one, which should be rejected for that reason? An ableist philosophy of sport seems like one of exclusion for any group or individual lacking the requisite abilities. How are we to answer that charge? Further, I developed an account of fairness in Chapter 5 around the notion of agency and the consent an athlete gives in playing a game. Suppose athletes are unwilling to consent to a sporting encounter because they think a competitor is not the right sex. Does that give them a right to withdraw consent and object that the contest is unfair, for instance where a shared understanding of the gender divide has been violated? These questions will have an answer below.

The Argument for Inclusion

Before we come to concrete cases, we would do well to consider the ethics of inclusion in the abstract. We need an understanding of the positive case for inclusion so that we can adopt it as a framework and apply it to the cases of disability and gender, or any future groups under threat of exclusion. Some of the materials for an argument have already appeared, but we can add to them and organise the points into an explicit, though informal, argument. The argument I suggest is as follows:

1. Every agent has an equal right to flourish

2. Flourishing comes from the development and exercise of capacities

3. Participation in sport contributes to the development and
   exercise of capacities

Therefore, every agent has an equal right to participation in
sport.

    I should say something in explanation and defence
of each premise. After that, I will be applying the conclusion.
    The first premise provides the normative compo-
nent of the argument since it talks of rights, and without this
we would not have the normative content of the conclusion.
A right is what I would call a thick normative concept. I am
taking *ought* to be the thinnest normative concept where
thicker normative concepts are specific ways in which something ought to be, carrying subsidiary implications. I take it
that a right is an entitlement: something that ought to be
accepted and respected in virtue of meeting certain basic
conditions. In the case of premise 1, the condition to be met
is being an agent, which means that most human beings
would have this right and possibly some animals too.
A human might not be a moral agent if they have lost their
capacity of agency, such as if they are in a deep persistent
vegetative state, but they would still be a moral patient. Such
a person can do no right or wrong but right or wrong can
still be done to them. Now I do not have an argument to offer
in defence of premise 1. It is an egalitarian premise based on
the idea that all agents have equal worth. This is a commonly
held view, however, and is found in a number of ethical
systems, even if only implicitly. I am thinking of Kantian
ethics, in which each person is to be regarded as an end in
themselves and not a means, and also Bentham's

utilitarianism in which each person's pleasure is to be given equal weighting in a felicific calculus. Anyone who has an inegalitarian conception of ethics is welcome to get off the bus now.

Premise 1 also names the good to which we have an equal right: namely, to flourish. Flourishing is a specific though only vaguely understood right. It concerns our development through time in which we grow and realise our potential to do well. At times in human history, there has been a struggle to meet basic needs or to gain much happiness at all. Premise 1 does not give us a right to flourish in such circumstances but concerns a distributive right: if there is some flourishing to go round, then we have an equal right to it. It should be shared.

Premise 2 offers a specific account of what flourishing consists in. This account of flourishing is informed by Amartya Sen's and Martha Nussbaum's capabilities approach to well-being (for example, their book *The Quality of Life*, 1993, and Nussbaum's *Women and Human Development*, 2000), added to my account in Chapter 1 of the development of abilities. One flourishes by gaining more and more capabilities, in learning new skills, in being free to exercise those skills, which prevents them from being lost, and so on. Of course, not everyone will be in a position to flourish throughout their whole life. Once we get beyond a certain point, we tend to lose abilities and go into a decline. Even here, we could think of a relative flourishing, where one is encouraged and helped to do as much as one can, consistent with one's health. While my concern is primarily with sport, the premise applies absolutely generally.

Someone flourishes when they learn a foreign language, how to bake bread, and to be good at building personal relationships. As I have already indicated, I do not see a major divide between the notions of ability, capacity and capability. They are all about what we can do.

Premise 3 applies this stance to the case of sport. It does not say that participation in sport is the only way in which agents can flourish through the development of their capabilities. Sport is just one way in which we can do so and, as we have seen already, this way is particularly good for physical flourishing. In many cases of sport, there is also a mental and personal flourishing that accompanies the physical one. As my account of learning how to dive in Chapter 1 showed, I felt a sense of achievement in conquering my fear and consequently feel a little less afraid of future physical challenges. My physical development was also my personal development. I need not go into greater detail on premise 3 since much of what has already appeared in this book supports it.

The conclusion that follows from these premises tells us that inclusion in sport should be the default. Moreover, it also tells us that exclusion from sport would need a justification that essentially challenged one or more of the premises or argued that they do not apply in the case at hand. Perhaps one would want to exclude someone from sport on the ground that they are not an agent or because the sport in question does not contribute to human flourishing at all or because the account of flourishing is wrong. I cannot stop others from mounting such arguments, though they would have a difficult job. It is hard to see how someone could want to play sport without being an agent. And a physical activity that did not contribute to flourishing (such as gladiatorial combat) is unlikely to be granted or retain the status of sport. I do not quite take it as an analytic truth that sport contributes to human flourishing, but I do take it that all sports do, as a fact of institutional practice. The capabilities approach to flourishing is perhaps the easiest premise to attack, since that is based on a philosophical theory and there can be rival theories. For now, however, I will say that the argument is safe enough and we should proceed to look at some specific cases.

Disability

The argument for inclusion establishes the principle that sport should be for all. We know historically, however, that sport has not been for all and there remain many barriers for people within certain groups. In the case of disability, the success of the Paralympics should not obscure the fact that disability sports have a relatively short history and have received less attention and commercial investment than male non-disability sports. The case for inclusion in sport made, I nevertheless want to consider two issues that come out of disability sport, which concern our conception of ability and sporting segregation. The latter also applies in the case of women's sport.

First, ability, and it is here that I shall address any charge of ableism misdirected against the theory of sport I have developed over the course of this book. Ableism is usually take to mean discrimination in favour of able-bodied people, but I have some caution in adopting this definition since it contains one of the very points I wish to challenge: that some people are able and others are not. Let me explain.

There are two ways in which disability could be understood: an absolute conception and a relative conception. The medical model is an example of an absolute conception; the social model is an example of a relative conception. An absolute conception says that there are advantageous abilities that some people lack, such as the ability to see or the ability to walk. An implicit assumption is that anyone would want to have these advantages if they are without them. This is a negative conception, which the term 'disability' sometimes seems to carry: it is at least negative in the sense that it is about what you do not have rather than what you do have. If we see sport as being about the development and exercise of abilities then it might seem to follow that privation of a human capacity is a defect of some sort, coupled with an idea of inferiority or lesser worth. These are very problematic notions to apply to a human being.

I want to reject this absolute and negative conception of disability entirely. Instead, a relative conception accepts differences between people without taking these as a ground for judgements of inferiority. A disability, rather, exists only in comparison to the abilities of others. It is not an intrinsic characteristic of any one person. Disability is instead socially constructed in the sense that no solitary creature, that was one of a kind, could count as disabled since there would be no others with whom to compare.

There are some living creatures with abilities we do not have. Bats can sense through echo location, for instance. We are not disabled through lack of this ability. Every creature has only a finite number of abilities so there are always many abilities that they lack.

Furthermore, a disability is not a real feature in the sense that, if it is anything, it would have to be a negative property, and negative properties are problematic. I have the real property of being 1.78 metres tall. It is true, then, that I am not 1.8 metres tall but I do not have a real property of being not-1.8 metres tall. It makes most sense to understand being not-1.8 metres tall as being about a (positive) property that I don't have rather than a (negative) property that I do have. We all have abilities and some have more than others. That someone lacks an ability can only be sensibly maintained as a relative judgment. No one would bother saying that Usain Bolt has a disability of being unable to jump to the moon since, while he does not have that ability, nor does anyone else. Our judgements of disability are relative to the abilities that other people commonly have.

Disability is socially constructed in a more practical sense, too, which we will see applies very immediately to the case of sport. The lack of an ability is problematic only because we have a built environment and social practices designed by and almost entirely for the group of people who consider themselves able-bodied. Indeed, this is what makes it problematic for people with disabilities. Multi-storey buildings have stairs and sometimes poor or no lifts for wheelchair users. Accommodations for disability are often an afterthought that the able-bodied majority neglect in our ableist society. Likewise, we have institutionally constructed sports requiring abilities that most but not all people have. Without adaptations, these sports will exclude those who lack that required ability. Nevertheless, it is hard to think of a case where adaptations are not possible at all. To take an impressive example, it might be thought that archery is a sport that has no option but to exclude blind people. There is, however, visually impaired archery (I have reservations about the term 'impaired', since it suggests a defect and an absolute conception of disability), which uses a variety of techniques for 'spotting' the target. After all, the skill of archery has never really resided in seeing the target but in coordinating one's actions with respect to that target and having the steadiness of technique to maintain that aim.

It is possible, then, to defend a non-ableist conception of sport to which the argument for inclusion applies. Whatever abilities one is capable of developing, access to and participation in sport is one way of flourishing as an agent. There are abilities that some people do not have and are not in a position to develop, but it is still the case that they should have equal opportunities to develop the abilities that they do have. Where accommodations can be made, they also may have the opportunities that achieve the prelusory goal of the sport by exercising another ability that achieves the same end, as in the case of spotting the archery target without sight. It follows, by the inclusion argument, that if we deny people access to sport on the grounds of their disability, then we are violating their rights.

How, though, should we organise access to sport in the case of disability? Clearly, there are different ways in which it could be organised, and this brings us to the issue of sporting segregation. One form of organisation would be to let everyone compete against each other irrespective of level or ability. Paralympism is, after all, a relatively new development in disability sport. The first proper Paralympic games did not occur until 1960 and then only on a very small scale compared to what we know now. Prior to that, some people with disabilities did compete in the Olympics and there was no reason for them not to since the lack of a particular ability might have no relevance to their chosen sport. For example, Lis Hartel won a silver for Denmark at the 1952 Olympics in dressage where the paralysis in her legs did not impede her equestrian participation enough to prevent success.

Nevertheless, this negligible effect of disability would only apply to some sports. Hartel could excel at that event but, in some sports, the limited use of her legs would have been a major disadvantage. Nor should we rule out the possibility of an accommodation putting an athlete at an advantage over those competing without the accommodation. There is, then, an argument from fairness for separating disability sports from non-disability sports, and this is the situation that, to a large extent, we currently have.

There are still exceptions, of course, and we will see that disability differs from gender in this regard. First of all, it is still possible for an athlete with a disability to compete in a non-disability sport if they require no accommodation. This is like Lis Hartel's case, where the ability that is absent is not one required for success in the sport. An athlete might not even declare a disability if it is deemed irrelevant to the sport in question, as would be the disability of dyslexia for most sports, for example. Second, however, we have seen that athletes with disabilities have been allowed to compete against non-disabled athletes where the accommodation that allows them to compete is deemed not to give an unfair advantage. A high-profile instance of this was when Oscar Pistorius competed in the 2011 athletics World Championship, winning a medal, and then the 2012 Olympics (I feel I have to acknowledge at this point that Pistorius is now a convicted killer). His participation came only after a legal dispute with the International Association of Athletics Federations (IAAF) over whether his artificial running blades gave him an unfair advantage. Presumably, an accommodation that left the athlete still at a disadvantage would have been less objectionable to the IAAF, but it was the thought that the accommodation could have made a disabled athlete better than a non-disabled one that was contentious.

This concern – that an accommodation that might help an athlete with disability beat an athlete without one – is problematic to an extent. One could think that there is nothing in principle wrong with disabled athletes winning against non-disabled ones. We will see a similar contention in the case of gender. Disability might have an additional aspect, however, that we do not get for the issue of gender. There is a possibility that the accommodations for disability get better and better as technology improves; for example, if running blades become more advanced. The issue then is that the contest is not merely an athletic one but also a technological one. The fear would be that the technology produces enhanced humans equipped for advantage. It is for this reason that the sporting authorities have preferred an approach of segregation: keeping athletes with disability in their own disability sports. Those sports can then be codified, keeping control of the required accommodations and also control of the classification system, where disabilities can be separated according to their degree of impact on performance.

A fairness argument is at work, here, which we will see is applied less successfully in the case of a gender separation in sport. In the case of disability, the presumed basis of segregation is that it would be unfair for a disabled athlete to compete against a non-disabled one since, presumably, they would have too little chance of winning (although Pistorius challenged that assumption). One wonders, then, what the authorities are hoping to achieve in policing the boundary between disabled and non-disabled. Is it to give everyone an equal chance of winning? That is manifestly not the case. Even in non-disabled sports, some athletes are far better physically equipped for their sport than others. Sport is all about showing one's different levels of ability. Nevertheless, I accept that it could be unfair to expect some athletes with disabilities to compete against some of the best without disabilities to the extent that it could be perceived as a lack of acknowledgement of the lived experience of disability.

Women's Sports

I move now to sport and gender where we will find that some of the same issues will arise. For example, we will see that here too the sporting authorities police and enforce a divide and operate sport in a segregated way. It is not just the institutions of sport that do this. A gender divide is a requisite of the broader social arrangements within which sport is situated.

The parallels between disability and gender, in their treatment by sporting organisations, are rather striking. Women too have been included in sport relatively late. The first women's Olympic marathon wasn't until 1984 and the first 10,000 metres was as late as 1988. The FIFA Women's World Cup did not begin until 1991, some sixty-one years after inauguration of the men's competition. Women's football had been hugely popular in England during and after World War I, with so many men away and lost at war. A crowd of 53,000 was attracted for Everton against Liverpool. Nevertheless, the women's game was banned in 1921 and the men's game then started to grow again. (Was the women's game banned *in order* that the men's could grow?) Women's boxing was admitted to the Olympics only in 2012 after a long history in which it was in many places banned. Other events have a longer history of women's participation but sometimes with women playing a less demanding version of the men's game: for example, only playing three sets in tennis instead of the men's five, or having a slower course in downhill skiing.

Application of the argument for inclusion tells us that women, of course, have a right to flourish through participation in sport. The history of women's sport suggests, however, that the authorities have been slow or reluctant to grant this right, indicating that they have treated being a woman as akin to a protected category, like disability, and requiring accommodation.

Such an interpretation is only confirmed by recent debates concerning women with differences of sex development and transgender women. Women's sport is sometimes understood as lagging behind men's in a purely athletic sense. Records and times in comparable events show that there is at least a *prima facie* case for this. At the time of writing, the men's world record at 100 metres is 9.58 seconds while the women's is 10.49. In the javelin, the men's record is 98.48 and the women's is 72.28 metres. There is no need for further examples since they are not in short supply. There are various reasons why sport might be segregated into separate men's and women's events, but one view is that in most sports there is a difference in potential performance levels that comes with gender, the assumption being that in almost all cases men are will outperform women. If women are to have a chance of victory, then, they had better not compete against men. Again, there is an argument of fairness in favour of this segregation, then, which is that it would be unfair for women to compete against men since the women would be at a disadvantage purely in virtue of being women. The concern over whether some entrants properly count as women can be understood in this context. If a particular athlete is not 'really' or 'fully' a woman, then they might benefit from an unfair advantage. The category of woman within sport is to be protected and its boundaries policed to prevent anyone from straying into women's sport who does not properly belong in there and taking some of the glory that had been reserved for 'real' women.

I have tried to present in a fair light what I take to be the argument for excluding some individuals from women's sport. This is where they are not thought properly to qualify as women. The most common such cases are because they have differences of sex development or are transgender. Nevertheless, I will defend the opposite view and mount an argument for inclusion specifically for women in these groups. I will make use of two articles: Jennifer Doyle's 'Capturing Semenya' (2016) and Dvora Meyers' 'The Obsession with Caster Semenya's Body Was Racist from the Very Beginning' (2019).

We should start with a diagnosis of the problem. I have granted that, *prima facie*, men have hitherto outperformed women in sport. This is taken as a basis, on the ground of fairness, for keeping anyone out of women's sport who does not fully qualify as a woman. However, whether it is natural or inevitable that men outperform women should be questioned. It is clear, as I summarised above, that overall men's sport has had a huge head start over women's. Men in the modern era have been encouraged to develop their athletic excellences while women have not. While strides have been made, we can expect women's sports to have a time lag in their development especially as the unequal treatment of men and women in sport is ongoing. There are vast differences in investment and resourcing between men's and women's sport perpetuating the inequality. During the Covid-19 pandemic, for instance, men returned to elite sport as soon as was possible. This was the case in English football. The women's version of the game was not restarted until much later. It might be claimed that there were good commercial reasons for men's sport to return, since it can generate so much from TV revenues. Perhaps this also explains the hugely disproportionate investment in men's sport compared to women's. This is far from inevitable, however. TV audiences have grown for women's sport where their broadcast was properly promoted and prioritised, such as the most recent Women's World Cup in football. Of course, one could say that the investment in women's sport should follow only after it has generated the revenues to pay for it. This was not historically the case in men's sport, however, where there have always been investments in coaching and infrastructure on the basis of promise of future revenue.

Might one say that men's sport started already from an advanced position since men are naturally stronger, fitter and more competitive? The problem is that there is no way to prove this and it is almost certainly false. The recent history of sports development has shown that women have been treated as inferior in several ways, revealing that the institutions of sport manifest patriarchal power structures. The problem, then, is that there have been few periods in known history where patriarchy has not held sway. Seldom have women been encouraged to develop the physical characteristics of strength and power and the dominating mentality of ruthlessness, which could then be a basis of athletic excellence. One exception was ancient Sparta where women had just as brutal a life as men and were prepared for participation in war. The place of women now, however, is more a result of millennia of patriarchal social systems that have not prioritised the development of women's capacities. If women are not matching the sporting achievements of men, then, it is not the fault of women but of men.

Patriarchy is a system of sex-based power imbalance. How do differences of sex development and transgender athletes relate to this historical and ongoing patriarchal dominance? The reason is that it is integral to any patriarchal system that it maintains a myth of sharp gender boundaries. If power is to reside with men, then it had better be clear what a man is. Any blurring of the boundary between men and non-men is a potential incursion into the stronghold of power. We have advanced enough to know, however, that matters are not quite so clear-cut. Socially constructed gender is understood as more significant than biological sex. The binary divide is crumbling. Many people still identify as unambiguously man or woman, but not all do. Some people are non-binary. It is not simply that there is now a third intersex category to accommodate, though. The differences between men and women fall on a spectrum, resistant to any sharp boundaries and classification.

These issues have affected South African middle-distance runner Caster Semenya more than anyone else in recent years. Semenya has never had any doubt that she is a woman and throughout her career has competed in women's races. It is not through her own choice that she is at the centre of these debates. However, objections have been raised repeatedly concerning her sex status and she has been subjected to many forms of sex testing. One assumes that this has been against her will since some of the testing is of an intimate and humiliating nature, but she also knew that refusal to submit to such tests could lead to her being deemed ineligible for competition. This is immediately discriminatory since no competitors in men's sport are ever subjected to sex testing.

It is worth considering also why some women, but not others, are subjected to sex testing in the first place. Any initial suspicions that an athlete is not 'really' a woman are based on visible phenotypic traits. In other words, the athlete looks 'manly', according to the opinions of the sporting bodies. But what does that mean? Being powerful? Being tall? Having a developed musculature? These are characteristics that tend to produce sporting success, which is what all participants aim at. Why, then, is eligibility called into question, and the prospect of sex testing raised, for having those advantages and being a success? Like Semenya, Usain Bolt was also bigger and more powerful than his rivals but his physical advantages were regarded as something to be celebrated and admired rather than feared and questioned. Perhaps this is where Semenya really threatens patriarchy. She is not what a woman is *supposed* to be. She has a strength and power that men wish to reserve for themselves.

Suppose an athlete does submit to sex testing in order to save her career. What do we then find? A problem here is that there is no one definitive marker of sex. An intimate inspection might not be decisive since some people have ambiguous sex organs. What then? Not everyone has either XX or XY chromosomes. Since neither of these could show

127

Semenya to be not a woman, the authorities (in this case the IAAF) looked at Semenya's testosterone levels. Her levels are higher than most other women though it was not disputed that this level was naturally occurring. Nevertheless, the IAAF ruled that Semenya must take hormones to medically alter her testosterone levels in order to retain eligibility. This ruling was declared illegal by the Court of Arbitration in Sport (CAS), however, on a number of grounds. One was that it was discriminatory since no man who has a naturally high level of testosterone would be asked to medically reduce it to the same level as his opponents. Even more to the point, the IAAF had not produced sound evidence (mainly because there is none) showing that testosterone levels deliver a sporting advantage (see Cordelia Fine, *Testosterone Rex*, 2017, and Rebecca Jordan-Young and Katrina Karkazis, *Testosterone: An Unauthorized Biography*, 2019). This verdict was also appealed and overturned on the basis that some discrimination is necessary. We await the case's next step, scheduled for the Swiss Federal Tribunal.

Subverting the Gender Norms

We see a number of norms applying to women's sport that do not, then, apply to men. Unusual strength and power is celebrated in men's sport. In women's it is feared and viewed with suspicion. Semenya subverts patriarchal ideals of femininity. She is too tall, too powerful, too good. The authorities' response, to use Kate Manne's phrase, is to say 'Down Girl' (*Down Girl: The Logic of Misogyny*, 2018). To add a twist of intersectionality to the debate, Jordan-Young and Karkazis have argued that eligibility concerns in women's sport are also racist since the athletes under suspicion and affected by rulings are disproportionately black and from the global south. Black women athletes especially do not conform to the expectations white men have of femininity. Gender is socially constructed and a powerful voice in that social construction belongs to white men of the global north.

Differences in development is one thing. Do we need to add more to cover the case of transgender athletes? Transsexuality has aroused something of a moral panic generally and sport is often a focus of this panic. There are objections to women who have transitioned entering sport where it is felt that they retain some physical advantages from their pretransition life. An instance we can cite is world champion cyclist Veronica Ivy, who is also a philosopher and activist. She sometime races bearing the slogan 'Sport is a Human Right'.

Ivy has ambitions to be the first openly transgender Olympian, but it has not been an easy path. Some voices have expressed concern about her physical stature even though there is no demonstration that anything about her bodily characteristics advantages her performance. She is taller than many of her competitors, for instance, but in a sport where height is not thought to be a significant advantage. Perhaps the biggest risk a transgender athlete runs is being too successful in that success is the point at which one's eligibility is most likely to be called into question. The perceived violation is again where the gender norms are subverted. The public rationale for exclusion is so that women can be protected against illegitimate entry. However, this argument itself is a manifestation of patriarchal power. Its power rests in the premise that women's sport is meant to be weaker than men's. The premise can be challenged; and this is what makes women's sport political in a way that men's sport is not. As Jennifer Doyle says:

> Women's sports is not a defensive structure from which men are excluded so that women might flourish. It is, in fact, the opposite of this: it is, potentially, a radically inclusive space which has the capacity to destroy the public's ideas about gender and gender difference precisely because gender is always in play in women's sports in ways that it is not in men's sports (with a few exceptions – e.g. figure skating). Because men have been so committed to the 'end of women's sports' for so long, women's sports thrives in the zone of destruction. It has its own character thanks to the gender trouble at its origin. If women's sports has one job that really is different from men's sports, it is the destruction of sex/gender difference. Men's sports (with a few exceptions which prove the rule) reinforce ideologies of gender difference. Women's sports destroy them.

Women's sport is in a position, then, to be inclusive. If it is so, it can challenge a gender divide that is the basis of patriarchy. It can subvert the norms of femininity that limit women's power. Women should be free to develop their own athletic excellences without gendered constraints. Inclusivity, and a destruction of the divide, stands to benefit women. Doyle notes how mixed-gender competitions are discouraged and dismissed by the patriarchal institutions of sport. An acknowledged 'problem' is that women who compete against men can produce better performances in doing so, through using men as pacemakers, for instance. As a result, times secured in mixed-gender events cannot count for Olympic qualification nor as records for women. Alternatively, big marathon races stop women running alongside men by having women start earlier. It looks like there are active efforts to discourage women raising their game to the levels achieved by men. Downhill skier Lyndsey Vonn has made this point, asking to ski the men's course, which is faster. She was not allowed to do so. After all, what if she could ski faster than the men! How much would this threaten patriarchy?

The account of consent that I developed in Chapter 5, as a basis for fair play in sport, might be raised here as an objection to inclusion. I conclude in favour of the inclusion of trans women in women's sport since the threat they pose is to patriarchal norms of gender, more than to other women. Doesn't my account of consent imply that other competitors have a right to withdraw their consent if they are opposed by a trans athlete? I argued that consent was granted on the basis of a shared understanding of the rules of the sport. If one athlete believes that the shared understanding does not include participation by trans athletes, can they not exercise their agency and declare the competition unfair? One could easily see this argument being advanced by someone who objected to competing against a trans opponent.

The original pro-trans verdict need not change, however. Of course, any athlete is free to withdraw from the competition at any time and for any reason. Participation in sport is always a voluntary matter. What this does not mean, however, is that athletes can vote another participant out of the competition. A right to withdraw is not a right to force someone else to withdraw. The governing bodies of the relevant sport have a powerful voice in determining the shared understanding of the sporting engagement. If they rule that trans athletes may compete, then those athletes are at liberty to do so even if others withdraw. Despite some anti-trans voices within those sporting institutions, they would be right to include trans athletes. The argument for inclusion shows that participation in sport is a right: as Veronica Ivy says, sport is a human right.

What Sport Could Be

In the past six chapters I have offered an account of the place of sport in human life. We are physical beings who flourish when we develop our capacities. Sport focuses especially on our physical being and, through competitive engagement with others, encourages the optimal display of those capacities. Sports are the codified forms of physical games. In many cases, codification has a purpose of making those sports attractive to watch, since there is a commercial gain from doing so. Sport has an ethically ambiguous status. Athletes are typically on the wrong end of an exploitative relation, incurring harms of various kinds. Nevertheless, sport can contribute to our flourishing and on that basis ought to be inclusive. Under current arrangements, however, sport has failings, both historical and current, that have erected barriers to inclusion.

Sport is a product of the social arrangements within which it is situated. Our exploitative world has produced an exploitative sport, full of the harms and vices that we are willing to inflict on each other. This can and must change.

We stand on the brink of an urgent social reconstruction. The environmental crisis, economic instability, global pandemic and the Black Lives Matter movement are catalysts for a major upheaval in human culture. It is time to think of new ways of organising our social relations. With that will come a new relationship to sport. We should now consider what an ideal sport could be. If we change the world in the right way, we could have a sport that is non-discriminatory, non-patriarchal, open and inclusive, that places human flourishing, freedom and happiness at the centre, with no abuse, no violence, no cheating, no exploitation, and where the competitive encounter of self and other is reward enough. Sport could be all this and more, if we make it so.

FURTHER READING

Here are some books that the interested reader can pursue if they want to discover more about the philosophy of sport. The list begins with two general books about philosophy of sport that will give a broad overview and then proceeds to some special topics and sports.

Heather Reid (2012) *Introduction to the Philosophy of Sport*, Lanham, Maryland: Rowman & Littlefield

This is a very good introduction to the philosophy of sport by one of the leading academics working in that field with sections on metaphysical, ethical and political aspects of sport together with a consideration of sport's history and heritage.

Emily Ryall (2016) *Philosophy of Sport: Key Questions*, London: Bloomsbury

Approaches sport through a series of philosophical questions, supplemented with interviews of leading philosophers of sport and study questions for the student. Topics include the nature and value of sport, the sporting body, aesthetics and ethics in sport.

Sigmund Loland (2002) *Fair Play in Sport: A Moral Norm System*, London: Routledge

Develops a theory of good sport based on an acceptance of a fairness norm and a play norm, which realise even competitions, open outcomes and unpredictability. These are needed for good sport to secure a sweet uncertainty of outcome.

Stephen Mumford (2011) *Watching Sport: Aesthetics, Ethics and Emotion*, London: Routledge

A consideration of the philosophical issues around watching sport rather than playing sport. Explores issues in aesthetics, ethics and philosophy of emotion since these are depicted as three of the main reasons to watch sport.

David Papineau (2017) *Knowing the Score*, London: Constable

A leading analytic philosophy wanders through a range of subjects wherein sport and philosophy deal with similar problems and find similar solutions. The author shows what sport can teach us about philosophy and what philosophy can teach us about sport.

C. L. R. James (1963) *Beyond a Boundary*, London: Hutchinson

Possibly the greatest thoughtful book ever written about a sport. C. L. R. James is both a philosopher and a cricket enthusiast. James situates the sport within a wider social context, including a colonial heritage that shows sports contains ambiguities.

Stephen Mumford (2019) *Football: The Philosophy behind the Game*, London: Polity

A philosophical examination of the world's greatest game, which considers some of its key components: how teams can be greater than the sum of their parts, the vital role of chance, the importance of empty space and the motivation of victory.

Bernard Suits (2005) *The Grasshopper: Games, Life and Utopia* (2nd edition), Peterborough, Ontario: Broadview Press

Suits's book, published originally in 1978, has been hugely influential in philosophy of sport and can be understood as a great work of philosophy generally. Developing Socratic themes, Suits argues for the place of games within utopia. The uselessness of games reveals their intrinsic value.

Other Works Referenced

Associated Press (2018) 'Parkour Eyed for 2024 Olympics by Gymnastics Officials amid Complaints', NBC Sports, 21 December (https://olympics.nbcsports.com/2018/12/21/parkour-olympics-gymnastics/). Accessed 30.6.20.

Doyle, J. (2016) 'Capturing Semenya', The Sport Spectacle, 16 August (https://thesportspectacle.com/2016/08/16/capturing-semenya). Accessed 30.6.20.

Fine, C. (2017) *Testosterone Rex*, London: Icon

Hornby, H. (2008) *Uppies and Downies*, Swindon: English Heritage

Jordan-Young, R. and Karkazis, K. (2019) *Testosterone: An Unauthorized Biography*, Cambridge, Massachusetts: Harvard University Press

Manne, K. (2019) *Down Girl: The Logic of Misogyny*, Harmondsworth: Penguin

McNamee, M. (2008) *Sports, Virtues and Vices*, London: Routledge

Merleau-Ponty, M. (1962) *Phenomenology of Perception*, translated by C. Smith, London: Routledge (originally published 1945)

Meyers, D. (2019) 'The Obsession with Caster Semenya's Body Was Racist from the Very Beginning', Deadspin, 4 March (https://deadspin.com/the-obsession-with-caster-semenyas-body-was-racist-from-1832994493). Accessed 30.6.20.

Nussbaum, M. (2000) *Women and Human Development*, Cambridge: Cambridge University Press

Nussbaum, M. and Sen, A. (1993) *The Quality of Life*, Oxford: Oxford University Press

Simon, R. (2000) 'Internalism and the Internal Values in Sport', *Journal of the Philosophy of Sport*, vol. 27, no. 1: 1–16

Wittgenstein, L. (1953) *Philosophical Investigations*, Oxford: Blackwell

INDEX